Language and Logos
in Boswell's
Life of Johnson

Language and
Logos in Boswell's
Life of Johnson

William C. Dowling

PRINCETON UNIVERSITY PRESS

PRINCETON, NEW JERSEY

Copyright © 1981 by Princeton University Press
Published by Princeton University Press, Princeton, New Jersey
In the United Kingdom: Princeton University Press, Guildford, Surrey

All Rights Reserved

Library of Congress Cataloging in Publication Data will be
found on the last printed page of this book

Publication of this book has been aided by the Paul Mellon
Fund of Princeton University Press

This book has been composed in Linotype Baskerville

Clothbound editions of Princeton University Press books
are printed on acid-free paper, and binding materials are
chosen for strength and durability

Printed in the United States of America by Princeton
University Press, Princeton, New Jersey

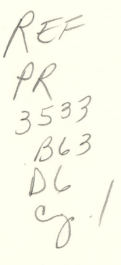

For Richard A. Lanham

CONTENTS

PREFACE

SURVIVAL in literary studies today, or in what one commentator has called the critical wars of the times, demands some acquaintance with contemporary critical theory, and I expect that most readers of the present study will have at least a passing acquaintance with the philosophical program of Jacques Derrida and with what is variously called "revisionist" or "antithetical" or "deconstructivist" interpretation (or, increasingly and by way of shorthand, "Yale criticism"). To such readers, my discussion of the narrative and thematic structure of Boswell's *Life of Johnson* is all too likely to appear a straightforward exercise in deconstructivist interpretation. It is not, and since it is not I must take the occasion of a preface to say something about my assumptions.

My aims in the following pages are avowedly syncretist—that is, I want among other things to reconcile theoretical claims that are most often seen to be in fatal opposition to one another, and to move interpretation closer to that stage of theoretical synthesis that is, as I see it, a happy inevitability in any case. My assumptions, at the deep level, are those of the objective or formal tradition in critical theory —the Anglo-American tradition of Richards and Empson and W. K. Wimsatt and Northrop Frye—and my claim is that these assumptions are not really irreconcilable with the newer assumptions of Derrida and the Yale critics. They demand explanation now only because they do exist at the deep level, beneath the deconstructivist surface of my argument.

The reconciliation or synthesis of rival theories is never, perhaps, either an easy or a straightforward enterprise—it is never, in any case, simply a matter of taking selected concepts from this theory and that and putting them all together as a new theory—and this is preeminently so when one comes to deal with the rivalry between objective and deconstructivist theory. My own approach, therefore, is as oblique as the situation demands: in a word, I see in deconstructivist theory not simply a theory but a radical critique of certain assumptions about literary structure associated with the objective mode of interpretation. It is the implications of that critique, already present but largely undeveloped in deconstructivist theory, that my argument concerning the structure of the *Life of Johnson* pursues to something like an end.

In a climate increasingly dominated by the clash of rival theories, there arises the question why such a critique, or another such critique, is either desirable or necessary. When we descend from the airy regions of abstract speculation to the world of literary works like the *Life*, do we not at least discover an adequate conception, the one great legacy of the objective or formal mode of interpretation, of literature as a sphere of reality demanding explanation in its own terms? Is it not at least true that interpretation may continue to view *Hamlet* or the *Life of Johnson* or *Middlemarch* or *Ulysses* as literary worlds complete in themselves?

The great problem with this line of argument is not itself theoretical. It is the problem posed in a dismayingly concrete way by the structure of the *Life of Johnson*, which has always resisted interpretation on these terms. The *Life* poses the problem because in its structure it challenges the notion of narrative continuity from which the notion of a literary world—when we are speaking of narratives like *Paradise Lost* and *Middlemarch* and *Ulysses*—implicitly derives. The *Life* is, in short, a narrative so obviously and radically discontinuous that it threatens every notion of the completeness and coherence of what we normally call the world of the work.

Yet though the problem is not theoretical in the usual sense, it is a problem with a heavy burden of theoretical implication. For in posing a challenge to conventional notions of continuity in narrative, the *Life* summons into the light of critical scrutiny that model of narrative structure always invisibly present when we speak of works like *Paradise Lost* and *Middlemarch* as essentially continuous. In this context, the problem is not the *Life* in its radical discontinuities but the set of assumptions silently in operation whenever we view narrative continuity as something only occasionally or incidentally problematic. The challenge of the *Life* is to the entire notion of continuity in narrative structure.

My purpose in the present study is to show in just what terms the *Life* poses this challenge, and what deeper thinking about literary structure it demands of us. The issues are many, and simultaneous, and complex. Yet a preliminary view of what is involved can be gotten, I think, from a brief and isolated consideration of one problem I shall later address at length, a problem associated with the concept of the narrator in literature. In works we call fictional, this is the problem of the imaginary speaker who tells the story, whether the highly visible and individualized storyteller like Robinson Crusoe or Tristram Shandy or the more universalized narrative voice of *Tom Jones* or *Pride and Prejudice*. In works like the *Life of Johnson* it is the problem that arises when we describe Boswell as a biographical narrator, or, indeed, when we invoke "Boswell" as the name of the voice telling Johnson's biographical story.

In the annals of critical theory, the concept of an internal voice in narrative represented a signal victory for formal or objective interpretation over an older genetic or biographical criticism. For it was at least intuitively obvious that no literary comprehension of *Robinson Crusoe* was possible until one had made the crucial distinction between Robinson Crusoe, imaginary misadventurer and dweller on an uninhabited island, and Daniel Defoe, a busy author who remained in London turning out numberless books and pamphlets. And it was only slightly less obvious that the narrator of *Tom Jones,* whose voice speaks from the page whenever the novel is begun again, belongs to a different sphere of reality than the historical Henry Fielding, the author and magistrate who died in 1754.

Whether or not we choose to retain a notion of "non-fictional" narrative as meaningful in purely generic terms—the terms, that is, on which we make meaningful use of such names as "epic," "tragedy," "comedy," and so on—the same reasoning gives us a distinction between Boswell as biographical narrator, an internal voice and presence in the *Life of Johnson,* and the author who died in London, seeing a third edition of the *Life* through the press, in 1795. This is the context in which the concept of a narrator or internal narrative voice represents the positive contribution of a theoretical battle otherwise fought in negative terms. The identification by Wimsatt, Beardsley, and others of an intentional fallacy at the root of genetic or historical criticism demanded that interpretation isolate in narrative an internal presence belonging solely to literary reality, and in the narrator it discovered the presence it sought.

If the concept of internal narrative voice seems unproblematic now (and it will appear wholly unproblematic except to those, today on the remote fringes of literary studies, who never learned the lessons of objective interpretation), it is because it solved so well the problem it was meant to solve, that of establishing a separation or ontological space between the imaginary world of literature and the world we variously call the ordinary, the everyday, the actual or the historical. To see that the concept remains intensely problematic, therefore, we must begin by recognizing its value, by seeing that the problems it raises are not of the older sort, all deriving from a confusion between literary reality and other realities, but of certain confusions contained in the very notion of internal voice in narrative.

One such problem, as I shall argue at length in Chapter One, lies in the notion of the narrator as a continuous presence in the work. In purely commonsensical terms, this is the problem of a narrator who is simply and obviously there from the beginning to the end of the story, who begins by introducing us to a world, continues by introducing us to certain figures in that world, and who then follows them to the end of that sequence of events we call the story. Whether the world is that of a long war fought before the walls of Troy, the heaven and hell and earth of Milton's epic vision, or the English villages and London streets of Fielding and Dickens, the narrator always hovers over its doings as a presiding presence, a mind or intelligence never absent from the reality over which it presides.

Given this scheme of an imaginary world, and of the narrator as a continuous presence, we seldom feel any discomfort on those occasions when narrators lapse into silence. Yet such moments of narrative silence are a feature of narrative from the beginning. Achilles speaks at length and Menelaus responds at length; Arthur and Bedivere pursue their sad dialogue and the narrator is wholly silent; in *Bleak House* the narrator simply disappears for long stretches and the story is told by its heroine in the first person. In every such moment of narrative silence there is a problem unresolved by our usual notions of narrative continuity.

As I shall later argue that the notion of mediation—of the narrator as a mediating presence between the audience and the world of the story—is both a common and a wholly unsatisfactory attempt to solve this problem, I need not summarize the argument now. The main point is this: in picturing the narrator as a mind or intelligence continuously present in the work, we are compelled to picture narrators as mysteriously present even when they are quite demonstrably absent or nonexistent. In a world composed solely of language they are somehow there even when not represented in their discourse. It is by imagining the narrator as a paradoxical presence-in-absence, a speech-in-silence, that we manage to retain our usual model of narrative structure.

This is precisely what the *Life of Johnson* will not allow us to do. Boswell as biographical narrator simply dematerializes for stretches of narrative time so long, stretches of narrative space so vast, that it is next to impossible to construe his absence as silence. And what occupies the narrative space thus vacated—letters, extracts from diaries, long conversation scenes cast in the form of dramatic dialogue, passages from literary works, historical documents, second- and third-hand accounts of Johnson, and much more—is altogether too heterogeneous to sustain a sense of Boswell's narration as nothing more than suspended discourse. So long as the lens through which we attempt to gaze at the *Life* is a conventional model of narrative structure, it is as though Boswell is being crowded out of his work by a bewildering diversity of competing materials.

Something, obviously enough, is wrong with our model here, something we cannot resolve by looking at the *Life* but only by scrutinizing carefully our own assumptions about narrative structure. And the answer that then suggests itself, or rather that is suggested by deconstructionist theory (and to a certain extent by phenomenological criticism as well), is that what is wrong is our usual notions of narrative continuity, of narrative silence as space occupied not simply by other orders of discourse but also, mysteriously, by the suspended speech of an absent narrator. The answer that suggests itself is that Boswell, in the moment when his narration ceases, really has dematerialized or disappeared. The absence of narration implies, on such a view, nothing less than the complete absence of a narrator.

Such a view demands that we abandon any notion of Boswell as a mediating presence, a narrative consciousness somehow occupying an imaginary space between an audience external to the story and the world populated by Johnson and Burke and Reynolds and Goldsmith and a hundred others, on the other side. It demands that we view the world of Boswell's consciousness not as something identical with or containing the world of the *Life*, but as a

limited world of discourse which now shrinks or dwindles
to become only one among a plurality of worlds contained
in the *Life*. It demands, even more urgently, that we envision the structure of the *Life* itself as a galaxy of such
worlds in relation to one another.

When we look at the *Life of Johnson* this way, a way so
powerfully invited by the otherwise vast and bewildering
structure of the work, we see simultaneously that what we
formerly termed "Boswell" or "the biographical narrator"
in the *Life* was really one order of discourse among others
in the text—discourse not only discontinuous with but existing as an *order* of discourse *by virtue* of its discontinuity
with other orders of discourse. Those terms "narrator" and
"Boswell," conjured up by a misleading model of narrative
structure, were nothing other than fictions of continuity or
presence invented to master the discontinuities of the text.
The problem of the *Life* in all its radical discontinuities,
then, is that it will not be mastered on these terms.

To conceive of Boswell's narration simply as one order
of discourse in the *Life*, of the world of his consciousness
simply as one world among a plurality of worlds, is to see
the dismaying heterogeneity of the *Life* separate into other
orders of discourse, other worlds. There is the epistolary
sphere of Johnson's correspondence, the transactions of a
mind *in* the world, the world of the great conversation
scenes, in which speech or conversation becomes itself a
world, the lonely and anguished domain of the *Prayers and
Meditations*, lying as a dark and spectral region beyond the
outward bustle and conviviality of the *Life,* and other
worlds as well. The study of the *Life* thus becomes a study
of relations among its worlds.

These are the terms on which I undertake to elucidate
the structure of the *Life* in the following chapters, and by
way of preliminary remark I need mention only one other
principle of structure that guides my interpretation. It is
the principle of antithesis, or antithetical relations among
that plurality of worlds contained in the *Life*. For it is not

simply that the *Life* is a work radically discontinuous in its structure, or that its very discontinuities point unwavering-ly to a plurality of worlds rather than a single world identi-cal with its narrator's consciousness, but that these worlds exist in subversive or antagonistic relation to one another.

As this is, once again, a point I shall later pursue in some detail, it need only be mentioned now. Yet every reader of the *Life* has been uncomfortably aware at one moment or another, I imagine, that its structure is not stable in the normal or benign sense, that the image of Johnson as an idealized moralist and sage is somehow at odds with that other Johnson who eats so voraciously that he per-spires with exertion, who mutters and gesticulates oddly in company, who is so prey to melancholy that he finds him-self in a paralysis of despair for weeks and months on end. It is a narrative logic of antithetical relations that allows us to see all this not as odd or inexplicable merely, but as meaningful in its own terms.

Since what I have said thus far is so obviously decon-structivist in its emphases, and since in the following chap-ters I shall be giving both a short exposition of deconstruc-tivist theory and a detailed demonstration of deconstruc-tionist interpretation, I want to be clear about one last matter. There is a tendency among critics who have only a superficial acquaintance with the theory to think of decon-struction as an interpretive activity, something one does *to* texts rather than something one sees *about* texts. Yet it is, as Hillis Miller well describes it, something one sees about texts after all:

> Deconstruction as a mode of interpretation works by a careful and circumspect entering of each textual laby-rinth. . . . The deconstructive critic seeks to find, by this process of retracing, the element in the system studied which is alogical, the thread in the text in question which will unravel it all, or the loose stone which will pull down the whole building. The deconstruction, rather,

annihilates the ground on which the building stands by showing that the text has already annihilated that ground, knowingly or unknowingly. Deconstruction is not a dismantling of the structure of a text but a demonstration that it has already dismantled itself.[1]

Whatever their truth about deconstruction as it is being pursued in various ways elsewhere, Miller's comments are precisely true of my own assumptions in seeking to elucidate in a new way the structure of the *Life of Johnson*. To explain the greatness of Boswell's great biography, it seems to me, must be to explain that plurality of worlds it has always contained, and to explain as well that dark light of antithetical relation in which the norms of one world are threatened or subverted by the norms of other worlds. The *Life* is not a massive and marmoreal literary monument overgrown with moss and old ivy. It is, as some readers at least have always known, a vital and exciting work of the literary imagination. My undertaking aims at nothing less than showing how and why this is so.

At the same time, I would be disingenuous did I not confess that the following pages have their own hidden agenda, one that reaches through the *Life* to certain abstract problems about literary structure. I chose to write about the *Life* because it has always fascinated and continues to fascinate me, and because I have been studying its narrative and thematic structure closely for over fifteen years. Yet the problems the *Life* exposes in its radical discontinuities are problems present in all narrative, less insistently perhaps, but yet insistently enough to demand that we empty our minds of outworn theoretical assumptions and begin to think anew. I write in aid of this enterprise as well.

While my major aim in what follows is always to throw new light into the vast and labyrinthine structure of the *Life*, then, I aim too to provide a partial grammar of dis-

[1] J. Hillis Miller, "The Critic as Host," *Critical Inquiry*, 3 (Spring 1977), 434.

continuity for dealing with other texts. For the central insight of modern literary studies, it seems to me, is that literature is not a miscellaneous collection of unrelated works but a universe of meaning to which every work of literature belongs. This is the context in which whatever is true of the *Life of Johnson,* if it is the truth, must be true of *Paradise Lost* and *Tom Jones* and *Middlemarch* and numberless other works at the same time.

My direct intellectual obligations in the writing of this study are limited and important. They are to Frank Brady, who guided my studies in Boswell and in critical theory when I was an undergraduate, to Walter Jackson Bate, who both in his published work and his conversation has had an immeasurable influence on my thinking about the *Life,* to Linda Dowling, who took time out from her own research and writing to discuss with me in detail every important problem in the writing of the book, and to Leopold Damrosch, whose searching criticisms of the penultimate draft led to its present form.

Another category of obligation is less easy to define. This study was conceived and partly written while I carried a full teaching load, amidst the usual departmental and administrative burdens of university teachers, and in a climate not always congenial to scholarship. I owe the psychic space that permitted me to work to a sustaining group of friends and supporters—James Barbour, Angela Boone, Patrick Gallacher, Anne and Russell Goodman, Peter White, Mary Bess Whidden, Hugh Witemeyer, Nathaniel Wollman— whose book this is too.

I wrote the study in its present form as a Fellow of the National Humanities Center in the academic year 1979-80, and seminars and discussions with the other Fellows did much to crystallize my argument. In particular, I owe thanks to Cleanth Brooks, Jon Moline, Chaim Perelman, and Paul Ricoeur for specific points that made their way

into the final draft, to David Falk for many hours of illu-
minating discussion of various theoretical problems, and to
Quentin Anderson for an uncompromising resistance to
everything structuralist and post-structuralist that, because
it always remained good-humored, led to several ultimate
clarifications. I wish as well to thank the staff of the National Humanities Center for support both moral and
practical. Thanks are also due to the editor of *Studies in
English Literature* for permisison to reprint portions of
Chapter Five which originally appeared in an article in the
Summer 1980 issue.

My greatest obligation over the last five years is registered
in the dedication to this volume. The intellectual influence
of Richard A. Lanham in the following pages will be evident to every reader familiar with his writings, especially
at the point in chapter four where the argument of his great
work *The Motives of Eloquence* is simply and unabashedly
adjusted to the demands of deconstructionist theory. What
the reader cannot see is the unwavering support he has
given me and my work over the years in those dark moments of solitary labor when it is a struggle to write or
think anything at all.

Language and Logos
in Boswell's
Life of Johnson

ONE

WORLD AND ANTIWORLD

ONE of the last great puzzles in the serious study of eighteenth-century literature is the vast and complex structure of Boswell's *Life of Johnson*. If recent years have brought considerable advances in our general understanding of Boswell's literary achievement—and this now includes the journals as well as the three narratives published during his lifetime—they have at the same time brought us only to the threshold of an understanding of the *Life*. The *Life*, which seems to enclose and body forth in its pages an entire literary age, a teeming world of thought and speech and action, of high intellectual and historical drama, may be said to stand in relation to later eighteenth-century English literature much as Joyce's *Ulysses* stands in relation to modern literature: it is a nexus, an ideal or abstract crossroads, of so much that is essential to its literary moment.

To say that *Ulysses* in some sense gives form to what we should want to call modern consciousness or modern sensibility is to introduce another puzzle: in what sense do the wanderings of Bloom and Stephen, the wise innocence of Molly, enact a drama we recognize as distinctively modern? In the case of the *Life of Johnson*, this sort of puzzle, at least, does not exist. The *Life* is not simply a work we range on our shelves with other great works of the eighteenth century, with *Tom Jones* or *Clarissa* or *The Decline and Fall of the Roman Empire*, for it encloses all those works: *Tom Jones* and *Clarissa* are precisely what are at issue when we hear, within the pages of the *Life*, Johnson debating with his company the relative merits of Fielding and Richardson; it is Gibbon, in the wake of the literary triumph marking the publication of the *Decline and Fall*, who along with Johnson and Boswell attends meetings of the Club.

In the same way, the *Life* may be said to enclose the larger intellectual and historical drama of the age to whose literature it belongs. To see Johnson's conversation in the *Life* as an abstract conflict with the freethinkers and philosophes of the European Enlightenment, with Voltaire and Rousseau and Hume and a hundred more, is inevitably to glimpse in the background the great sweep of ideas and events carrying Europe toward the upheaval of the French Revolution. To understand why Pope looms as so large a presence in the *Life*, a central character absent so to speak only by reason of his death, is to understand Johnson as a survivor of the Augustan moment, speaking, in a world where speech is itself a world, in accents growing daily more alien.

If we have begun to understand all this, it is paradoxically because we have learned to see Boswell's literary achievement in purely literary terms, to see that the world bodied forth in the *Life* exists on just the same terms, as problematic as literary reality itself, as the worlds of *Hamlet* or *Paradise Lost*. The older notion of the *Life* as a window on some actuality the atoms of which have long since dispersed, the idea of Boswell's biographical story as a mere document or record or transcript of "historical" reality, has given way to a perception of the *Life* as a self-contained world of motive and speech and action. The *Life* is a work we gaze not through but into, and it is this we mean when we say it bodies forth a world.

Yet to assert even this is to raise the problem of what we mean when we speak of the world of *Hamlet* or *Paradise Lost* or the *Life of Johnson*—indeed, of how we can speak intelligibly about the world of any literary work, or of literary works as composing the simultaneous order we call a literary universe. If we are doing anything more than employing crude or empty metaphors in such contexts, it is obvious that our terms must refer to something essentially true of the sort of reality embodied in literary works, or, at the furthest reach of implication, to something we intuitively perceive as being true about the ontological status of

4

literature as a whole. And our best evidence that this is so, that our terms are neither crude nor empty (and perhaps not even metaphorical), is that they function with perfect intelligibility in critical discourse; if everything behaves as though a sign had meaning, wrote Wittgenstein in the *Tractatus*, then it does have meaning.

When we consider the concept of a literary world in this light, a number of considerations arise. Some, however interesting in themselves, are tangential to my present concerns. The possibility that our use of the term "world" in critical discourse is not metaphorical, for instance—as though, possessed of some immediate sense of what *the* world is, we were led to speak of a world of *Hamlet* as one speaks of the warrior as a lion or the lady as a rose—suggests that we may be using the term much as the term "space" is used in physics or mathematics: as the relation between physical space and Hilbert's n-dimensional space is not metaphorical, one might argue, neither is the relation between our world and the world of *Hamlet*. Yet since it can also be argued that metaphor controls relations among such concepts at a deep level, such issues promise only to detain my inquiry.

The simple observation that "world" seems perfectly intelligible when we use it to describe *Hamlet* or *Paradise Lost* raises one possibility that, while it need not keep us, must not be overlooked. This is the possibility that the concept, by virtue of its intelligibility to those who pursue literary study, may be unanalyzable, that it belongs to what Michael Polanyi, in *Personal Knowledge* and other writings, calls the tacit dimension of our knowledge—in this case, of our knowledge about literature. For the student of literature, as much as any inquirer, is the inhabitant of a methodological universe, and in any such universe much of what is known is discovered, as Polanyi says, "by the observance of a set of rules which are not known as such to the person following them."[1] It may well be that the concept

[1] Michael Polanyi, *Personal Knowledge: Towards a Post-Critical Philosophy* (Chicago: The University of Chicago Press, 1958), p. 49.

of a literary world, governed by rules invisible to those of us who use them, belongs precisely to the tacit dimension of our inquiries into literary meaning.

Even should this turn out to be so, however, it would in no way frustrate my inquiry, for there remains the question—more than enough to go on with, so to speak—of what exactly it is about literary reality that makes the concept of literary worlds intelligible. Most immediately, we are likely to guess, the question directs our attention to what modern critical theory terms literary autonomy, with which we associate a conception of literature as a self-contained sphere of reality existing separate from anything we should want to call our world. The theory of literary autonomy, and the standard objections to various elements of the theory, are too familiar to demand much comment. What is significant to my purpose is that the theory, on some level at least, satisfies an intuition: the world of *Hamlet,* whatever we mean by the term, is not the same as our world.

Though we associate the theory of literary autonomy with the classic period of formalist critical theory (the period, roughly speaking, stretching from Warren and Wellek's *Theory of Literature* to Frye's *Anatomy of Criticism,* and including such masterpieces of theoretical inquiry as Wimsatt and Beardsley's *The Verbal Icon*), it is worth noting that attempts to account for literature as a sphere existing separate from ordinary existence, as embodying a reality apart from the ordinary world inhabited by successive generations of men, go back at least as far as Aristotle's *Poetics.* This, or something like it, is what Aristotle has in mind when he says that poetry is a higher and more philosophical thing than history, what Sidney means when he says that literature gives us a golden world and nature only a brazen one, what Shelley invokes when he calls poets the unacknowledged legislators of mankind.

From Aristotle's *Poetics* to the aesthetic doctrines of Wilde, that is, we may in some sense consider the long history of western poetics as being composed of related attempts to account for an intuition of literary autonomy, as revolving around the central problem of what we mean by literary worlds or a literary universe. Viewed in this light, the interest of various poetics is precisely the way in which they manage to draw attention to various features of the problem. Thus Blake's typically brusque assertion that every work of art is necessarily a perfect unity, like Coleridge's account of organic form, takes literary autonomy for granted and directs attention to something else, the internal coherence or self-containedness of the literary world.

In the same way, the aesthetic doctrines developed by Wilde a hundred years later merely assert the autonomy of the literary universe in more extreme terms than formerly. To a generation living in the shadow of the grim concluding remarks of Pater's *The Renaissance*, the tragic insubstantiality of human life viewed as "the concurrence, renewed from moment to moment, of forces parting sooner or later on their ways" made art, and especially literary art, appear in the light of a reality more substantial, more coherent and permanent, than human existence. Thus Wilde, in *The Critic as Artist*, describing the heroes of the *Iliad*: "Phantoms, are they? Heroes of mist and mountain? Shadows in a song? No: they are real. Action! What is action? It dies at the moment of its energy. It is a base concession to fact. The world is made by the singer for the dreamer."

A conception of literature as a permanent and timeless reality existing outside the flux of atoms and unstable perceptions we call human existence is, of course, as much a literary theme as a matter of poetics. Shakespeare's "not marble, nor the gilded monuments/ Of princes, shall outlive this powerful rhyme," expressing a thought already old at the time of Horace, represents literature meditating on its own autonomy, gazing outward at the flux and insubstantiality of the ordinary world. This is, roughly speaking, the perspective that Wilde has transformed into doctrine: to assert that the world is made by the singer for the dreamer is to say nothing other than that the world of literature is, during the short period we exist as conscious beings, the only real world we may inhabit. Not to see this, to assume that the purposeless flux we call the ordinary world is what is real, or that the world of the *Iliad* or *Hamlet* is shadow or mist or dream, is itself to live a dream.

In any such work as *The Critic as Artist*, then, we find ourselves poised on an invisible line between poetics and metaphysics, gazing outward from a certain conception of literature to a glimpse of the ultimate nature of things. And it is the innocence of that gaze, the readiness of writers like Wilde to make rather breathtaking claims for the centrality of art in human life, that makes aestheticism seem now, at best, merely an important cultural episode, and at worst a body of attitudes merely curious or quaint. Yet modern critical theory, though its ostensible concern is with method rather than metaphysics, has never managed to relieve itself of a certain metaphysical burden; though it does so in ways less daring than Wilde, ways more considered and complex, it is no less concerned to explain the ontological status of literature.

And yet there has been, in the twentieth century, a genuine revolution in literary studies, a development that separates us from Wilde as dramatically as Einstein's relativity papers divide the modern physicist from his eighteenth- or nineteenth-century counterpart working and living in the universe of classical or Newtonian physics. This was the gradual discovery of a method of interpretation—one might say, without overstating the case, the emergence of a new methodological universe—that projects literature as a state of affairs mirrored in propositions about literary meaning. And like Wilde's permanent and timeless world of literary reality, literature as projected by modern interpretation is self-contained, internally coherent, and complete.

To perceive the revolution in modern literary studies as a triumph of method—the method, roughly speaking, of formal or objective interpretation—is to assign a curious place to critical theory. For now one may see that the works of greatest theoretical import were not themselves theoretical: from I. A. Richards's *Practical Criticism* to Cleanth Brooks's *The Well-Wrought Urn* and beyond, they were the works that demonstrated, in a way that could be absorbed and used by students of literature, the method that projected literature as an objective state of affairs. When such works pretended to theoretical rumination, as in Richards's psychomechanical theory of literature as a sort of therapy for the central nervous system, they are likely to seem now slightly bizarre; it was on actual interpretation that they exerted so profound an influence.

In this context, such works as Warren and Wellek's *Theory of Literature* and Wimsatt and Beardsley's *The Verbal Icon* may be viewed as attempts to explain the results or consequences of the objective method in interpretation—not, that is, as breaking new theoretical ground, but as moving in the wake of a methodological breakthrough that was seen as needing theoretical justification. Thus, for instance, the long debate over any such issue as "the intentional fallacy" may be viewed as an a posteriori pondering of something that had already occurred: just as the notion of God as creator or originator of the physical universe became an expendable hypothesis at a certain point in the history of scientific method, the author, or authorial intention, had become unnecessary to explain the results of objective interpretation.

Yet the attempt to explain these results or consequences, though enormously suggestive in the first instance, was ultimately doomed to theoretical failure. To justify objective interpretation, theorists of the formal approach offered not arguments but metaphors, with the metaphorical assertion that the literary work was a "closed" form leading to endless controversy over such matters as whether interpretation could go "outside" the work in search of clues to its meaning, as opposed to remaining "inside" or adhering to an "internal" approach. The reason that such metaphors

9

carried conviction is that, even in the eyes of those who opposed an objective approach to interpretation, they referred in some obvious way to something actually occurring in literary studies.

In avoiding any direct assertions about the ontological status of literature, formalist theory seemed to have escaped the metaphysical implications always present in traditional poetics (though the early association of the theory with T. S. Eliot's poetics of impersonality and the "new criticism" urged by the poet John Crowe Ransom made clear its affinity with such poetics). Yet in reality the metaphor of "closed" form, as much as Sidney's Neoplatonic "golden world" of art or Coleridge's "organic form," was relentlessly ontological in its implications. If the metaphor insisted on something quite new, on literature existing in relation to interpretation as an objective state of affairs, it also asserted a very traditional view of the relation between literature and the world.

There is no great mystery, then, about why formalist theory at a certain point seemed exhausted, seemed outdated or limited or inadequate to explain what was occurring in actual interpretation. For the method that the theory aimed to justify in one sense needed no justification: just as physics after Newton needed no theory of physics, only the Newtonian paradigm and an established method of experimentation and hypothesis, objective interpretation needed no theory of interpretation to explain literature as a state of affairs or object of inquiry. The metaphors of formalist theory, along with their inescapable ontological implications, were never in any genuine sense confuted or supplanted; like all metaphors posing as axioms, they simply expired as vital theoretical imperatives, and survive now only as exhibits in the history of critical thought.

Yet the conception of literature as an objective state of affairs remains as central today as it was in critical theory twenty-five years ago, and is really what is at issue when we speak now of the literary work as a world in itself. If we now see Northrop Frye's *Anatomy of Criticism* as completing the formalist program in critical theory, for instance, it is less because of its theoretical contributions—e.g., Frye's demonstration that evaluative criticism was simply a prominent instance of the affective fallacy—than its assumption that literature exists as a universe within which every literary work may be seen as a world in relation to other worlds. This is precisely the universe literary study has undertaken to map and explain down to the present moment, a universe of infinite complexity and endless significance.

To describe literature in this way is, of course, to describe it as the object of inquiry primarily in Anglo-American literary studies. Yet even in Continental criticism an analogous conception of literature has, until very recently, guided inquiry: the criticism of Georges Poulet and the Geneva School, for all its superficial differences from Anglo-American interpretation, assumes the existence of literature as a self-contained sphere of reality (though for the Geneva School literary works are structures of consciousness to be explained in phenomenological terms). And structuralism posited a literary universe so similar to that of Anglo-American interpretation that Northrop Frye has sometimes been claimed as an unwitting structuralist.

More important, perhaps, is that serious challenges to the theory of literary autonomy have for the most part been compelled to operate in its terms. Thus Frederick Jameson's brilliant *Marxism and Form*, dismissing such critics as Caudwell and Goldmann as vulgar Marxists, begins by accepting something like the idea of self-contained and internally coherent literary worlds before attempting to dissolve them into that nexus of material relations that exists for Marxist doctrine as the only reality, the brute matter of history viewed in the blinding light of the material dialectic. For such attempts the theory of autonomy remains central, mistaken only as it demands to be explained in other terms.

When we speak today of the world of *Hamlet* or *Paradise Lost*, then, we are invoking a conception of literary reality that in a sense predated modern attempts to justify it in theoretical terms, and that has remained vital in the climate of theoretical exhaustion that has followed the demise of classical formalism. As a universe of literary worlds, literature exists in relation to objective interpretation much as the colorless universe of physics exists in relation to physics as a structure of inference and explanation: it is the state of affairs posited or projected by our explanations of literary meaning, a reality only glimpsed intuitively by western poetics from Aristotle to Wilde.

At the very least, this is to say that literature embodies a phenomenal reality and, just as important, that it compels us as students of literature to see all other spheres of reality in equally phenomenal terms. For a conception of literature as a state of affairs projected by objective interpretation avoids the *als ob* or either-or dilemma of traditional poetics: it is not that either the world of *Hamlet* or the state of affairs outside our window is real, the other merely a shadow or mist or dream, but that both are equally real, and real, as objects of perception and explanation, on analogous terms. To understand what we have come to mean by a literary world is simultaneously to see that, on some ultimate epistemological level, the only reality is the existence of separate realities or states of affairs.

To see the *Life of Johnson* in these terms is no longer, perhaps, controversial: to say that the *Life* embodies a world in just the same sense as *Hamlet* and *Paradise Lost* embody worlds is simply to assert its status as a work of literature, to observe that, whatever its interest for those concerned with "historical" reality, it may also be seen as belonging to the same universe as other literary works. And yet this is suddenly to raise a set of problems that remain invisible, at best obscure, when the *Life* is seen as document or record, for now one encounters the problem of how the

Life exists as a literary work, on what terms it embodies that phenomenal reality we call a literary world.

The problem may be seen in somewhat oversimplified terms as a problem of coherence—not whether the *Life of Johnson* is coherent as *Hamlet* or *Paradise Lost* are coherent, for that coherence is implied in what we mean by a literary world, but what precisely we mean when we say that the world of the *Life* is in its own terms coherent. The solution to the problem is not, obviously enough, to invoke the general notion of coherence we summon under the name of genre, to say that the *Life* embodies the conventions of biographical narrative in just the same way as *Hamlet* embodies the conventions of tragedy and *Paradise Lost* the conventions of epic, and that an awareness of these conventions provides us with a sort of Archimedean point from which to explore the full complexity of its world. The very idea of conventions, or structural resemblances among works quite different in themselves, presupposes some understanding of literary structure, and it is precisely the labyrinthine structure of the *Life* that challenges our usual notions of coherence.[2]

Seen in this perspective, the problem of the narrative structure of the *Life* might seem merely to be one of conventions not yet isolated, resemblances not yet seen as being resemblances. If the coherence of the world of the *Life* differs from the coherence of the worlds of *Hamlet* or *Paradise Lost*, may we not solve the dilemma by looking for its structural resemblances to other works—to, for instance, a work like the *Odyssey*, which it resembles in portraying its hero as making an epic journey, though through time rather than space?[3] (This is, after all, a resemblance Bos-

2 The *Life* does, however, obey certain narrative conventions that may be traced back to classical biography. See my essay, "Boswell and the Problem of Biography," in *Studies in Biography*, ed. Daniel Aaron (Cambridge: Harvard University Press, 1978), pp. 73-93.

3 "Boswell's central thematic purpose is to construct an epic, a

13

well strongly insists on in the opening pages of the *Life*.) Or, in its low-mimetic portrayal of eighteenth-century English society and manners, to such fictional narratives as *Tom Jones*? Or, in the great conversation scenes, so often cast in dramatic form, to seventeenth- and eighteenth-century comedy of manners?[4]

All such resemblances are crucial to our understanding of the structure of the *Life*, but the problem is that when we have got done cataloguing them we are no closer than before to seeing that structure steadily and whole. The reason that the *Life* eludes all such attempts to assign it a structural description (as the structuralists say) is precisely that it does not very much resemble any single work we have in mind. For all its affinities with the comedy of manners, the *Life* is not itself drama, nor is it, like the *Odyssey*, an epic in the conventional sense. It is not even, like *Tom Jones*, a continuous narrative, though that is perhaps the most general model I should want to invoke in attempting to understand its structure, and no model of discontinuous narrative—epistolary novels like *Clarissa* or *Humphrey Clinker*, say—seems very adequate to my purposes.

At the same time, I do seem to say something significant about the structure of the *Life* when I describe it as a discontinuous narrative (though this may put something of a strain on the normal use of the term "narrative"). For the structure of the *Life* poses a problem precisely because it is not narrative in any continuous sense. There are narra-

---

moral epic of heroic proportions, in which a man with greater strengths and weaknesses than ordinary, struggles with the problems of daily life and overcomes them. The remote model for that epic is the *Odyssey* with its archetypal journey pattern, the *Life* substituting a journey in time for one in space." Frank Brady, "The Strategies of Biography and Some Eighteenth-Century Examples," in *Literary Theory and Structure: Essays in Honor of William K. Wimsatt*, ed. Frank Brady, John Palmer, and Martin Price (New Haven: Yale University Press, 1973), p. 256.

4 See Sven Eric Molin, "Boswell's Account of the Johnson-Wilkes Meeting," *Studies in English Literature*, 3 (Summer 1963), 307-22.

tive portions, of course—roughly speaking, the portions of Johnson's story related directly by Boswell as narrator— but then there is a vast and confusing body of non-narrative elements: passages from Johnson's work and the work of other writers; letters to and from Johnson, involving a large and varied acquaintance, excerpted or included in their entirety; passages from the *Prayers and Meditations* and Johnson's private records; second-hand and third-hand accounts of Johnson from various sources; long scenes cast wholly in the form of dramatic dialogue; footnotes commenting on other footnotes; and much more.

The discontinuity of the *Life* does much to explain why an appeal to one or another literary model does so little to explain its structure. When I say that the *Life* has certain affinities with the *Odyssey*, for instance, or with such social novels as *Tom Jones*, I am really describing its narrative portions, Boswell's own perception of Johnson as a hero of epic proportions and of eighteenth-century English society as a low-mimetic milieu. The resemblance of the *Life* to a comedy of manners, on the other hand, refers most often not to its direct narration but to the conversation scenes, with their witty dialogues and comic reversals. The letters quoted in the text, so numerous and obviously significant as almost to tell a separate story in themselves, correspond in some oblique way to the model of the epistolary novel, and other elements point just as distractingly to other models, other worlds.

The overpowering suggestion, when one encounters so bewildering a diversity of elements, a discontinuity so pronounced as to make one wonder if the notion of continuity applies to the *Life* at all, is that an attempt to explain the coherence of the work through an appeal to other literary models is misguided at the outset, that it is the way one looks at the models themselves that demands scrutiny. For the source of frustration, obviously enough, is a puzzling relation between the structure of the *Life of Johnson* and that concept of a literary world which theory and interpretive method have made so unassailably familiar. In this context, to say that the *Life* in certain respects resembles a novel like *Tom Jones* is to raise the question of what one means when one calls *Tom Jones* a continuous narrative, or invokes the notion of narrative conventions to explain just what one means.

Now, however, the problem of what I mean by a literary world suddenly emerges as a new sort of problem. For it is not that I do not know what I mean when I speak of the world of *Hamlet*, but that I seem to know in very precise terms what I mean, that the concept is so universally established, so mutually intelligible to all schools of theory and interpretation, that I scarcely know how to begin to subject it to the sort of scrutiny my inquiry demands. Here again we encounter the dilemma raised by Polanyi's theory of inquiry itself: if the concept of a literary world belongs to the tacit dimension of our literary knowledge, is equally at work at some deep level in the Marxist criticism of Jameson and the phenomenological criticism of Poulet and the affective stylistics of Stanley Fish, then how should scrutiny begin?

The way out of the dilemma lies in an escape from the circle of theoretical unanimity, in an encounter with some theory of interpretation that altogether denies the existence of the literary world as a coherent and self-contained sphere of reality. And there is not far to seek: in the last few years, the deconstructivist approach of Jacques Derrida and his American adherents, among them such prominent scholars as Geoffrey Hartman and Hillis Miller, has mounted a radical challenge to every major assumption of Anglo-American criticism, and in particular to that concept of literary worlds crucial to my own inquiry. To see why the world of *Hamlet* does not exist for deconstructivist theory may at least suggest on what terms it exists within the framework of Anglo-American literary studies.

In such widely influential works as *De la grammatologie, L'écriture et la différance,* and *Marges de la philosophie—*

there are others equally influential, but these contain the heart of deconstructivist theory—Derrida has undertaken an enormously complex and ambitious philosophical program, one in which literary interpretation figures only as a prominent example of concerns more abstract, a kind of laboratory in which Derrida works out a general theory of meaning or signification. Yet because deconstructivist theory emerged from structuralism, and because structuralism at every stage has looked to a linguistic model, literature and the interpretation of literary meaning remain central to the deconstructivist program.

The philosophical implications of Derrida's program are beyond the scope of this inquiry, as is the style of interpretation currently being developed by such critics as Hartman and Miller. It is the narrow point of engagement between deconstructivist theory and the theory of autonomy underlying our usual notion of literary worlds that immediately concerns me, the sudden challenge to our assumptions that rises at a certain moment in Derrida's *La Dissémination*. The true object of interpretation, says Derrida there, is "une scène d'écriture dans une scène d'écriture et ainsi sans fin, par nécessité structurelle marquée dans le texte,"[5] a scene of writing within another scene of writing and so on without end, through a structural necessity marked in the text itself. There, in a single pregnant phrase, lies the challenge one seeks.

The challenge originates in Derrida's theory of the literary work as an empty nexus in a system of relations among works, of literature as corresponding to Saussure's famous model of language as a system in which "il n'y a que des différences sans termes positifs" (in which there are only differences without positive terms). Yet the real point of

---

[5] Jacques Derrida, *La Dissémination* (Paris: Seuil, 1967), p. 252. My attention was drawn to this passage by Edward W. Said's brilliant discussion of the Derrida-Foucault controversy in *Critical Inquiry*: Edward W. Said, "The Problem of Textuality," *Critical Inquiry*, 5 (Summer 1978), 694.

engagement between his larger theory and our usual assumptions lies in Derrida's view of what we are doing
when we assert, or show in the process of interpretation,
that the text—or, one may say equally, the world of the
work—has a fixed or discernible center of meaning. Jonathan Culler summarizes this portion of Derrida's argument
with admirable brevity:

> The study of structure is in this sense governed by 'a
> move which consists of giving it a centre, of referring it
> to a moment of "presence" or a definite origin'. This
> centre founds and organizes the structure, permitting
> certain combinations of elements and excluding others:
> 'the centre closes the play which it inaugurates and makes
> possible. . . . The concept of a centred structure is in fact
> that of limited or founded play'. This closure, it would
> be argued, testifies to the presence of an ideology.[6]

In speaking of the world of *Hamlet* or *Paradise Lost* or
Tom Jones, then, one is doing nothing more than confess-
ing one's own enslavement to a certain mode of reading,
to a system of convention—the totality of one's literary
education and the "ideological" pressures on it—no more
privileged than any other. Yet if interpretation can proceed only by positing one or another center of meaning,
and if all centers are equally arbitrary, why should it not
confess itself to be a futile enterprise, a pursuit of meaning
where only meaninglessness exists, and give itself over to
silence? The answer lies in another sort of interpretation,
a mode described by Roland Barthes in another passage
quoted by Culler, which rejects "the idea of a model transcendent to several texts (and thus, all the more so, of a
model transcendent to every text) in order to postulate
that each text is in some sort its own model, that each text,
in other words, must be treated in its difference, 'difference'

[6] Jonathan Culler, *Structuralist Poetics* (Ithaca, N.Y.: Cornell University Press, 1975), p. 244.

being understood here precisely in a Nietzschean or a Derridean sense."[7]

This is the mode of interpretation with which Derrida's followers in American criticism are now preoccupied, a style in which the critic, in an upward spiral of self-transcendence, subjects the false centers of his successive interpretations to a critique that exposes their inadequacy or falsity, until at last interpretation becomes a free play of signification, a Nietzschean participation in the innocence of becoming (it is Nietzsche's idea of the world as becoming, and of perfect freedom as participation in its process, that makes him so momentous a figure for Derrida and other theorists of deconstruction). At this level, the issue becomes the much-controverted question of whether interpretation is itself an autonomous activity; as such it does not concern me.

Something that does fall within the range of my present concerns, however, is Derrida's clairvoyant sense, present from the beginning of his program, that his theory involves a conflict of metaphysical systems. Our usual notion of a literary world, Derrida declares (and by extension all of western poetics back to Aristotle) derives from what he variously calls a "metaphysics of presence" and a "metaphysics of the *logos*," an impossible nostalgia for something lurking behind the word, a recoverable reality that interpretation vainly strives to bring back into our possession. Thus, in the alternative "metaphysics of absence" that deconstructivist theory proposes as a rationale for interpretation, the concept of the literary world is utterly annihilated.

There is this much truth in Derrida's attacks on the metaphysics of the *logos*: to read *L'écriture et la différance* or *Marges de la philosophie* alongside Aristotle's *Poetics* or Shelley's *Defence of Poetry* or Wilde's *The Critic as Artist* is to see as in a blinding light that much of western poetics is metaphysical speculation, and to see this moreover in just

[7] Culler, 242.

the terms in which Derrida wishes it to be seen. Are not Aristotle's idea of literature as embodying a universal reality, Sidney's golden world of art, Wilde's realm of permanence in the midst of tragic flux, are not these in some sense the haunted dreams of a nostalgia that longs to penetrate through language to a reality that exists independent of language, to a recoverable vision of things as they really and eternally are?

In a way much more limited, Derrida's attempt to demolish the metaphysics of the *logos* in favor of his own metaphysics of absence bears on the movement in modern critical theory I have identified with formalism. To the extent that the theory of literary autonomy could not avoid its own ontological implications, to the extent that it asserted a certain undefined relation between the world of literature and the ordinary world (and this is true almost no matter what one chooses to mean by "the ordinary world"), it participated in something very like that metaphysics of presence described by Derrida. The formalist metaphor of the literary work as a "closed" form with an "inside" and an "outside" testifies, after all, to nothing else.

To see what is really at issue here, one must suppose something that is not so in any direct sense, that Derrida's assault on the metaphysics of the *logos* is simultaneously an assault on the theory of autonomy associated with formalism—to imagine, that is, Derrida engaged in a direct dialogue with René Wellek or W. K. Wimsatt. For to narrow the focus of Derrida's argument in such a way as to bring it to bear on formalist theory is to expose a curious situation, one that can be appreciated only by those who understand and use the objective method of interpretation: the ontological or metaphysical implications are, so to speak, dispensable, and to demolish the theory is not to demolish the state of affairs—literature as embodying an autonomous reality—that the theory was constructed to explain or justify.

We have returned by a path somewhat circuitous, that is to say, to precisely that situation discussed earlier, in which formalist theory arose to explain the results or consequences of the objective method. Since it is the method itself that projects literature as a state of affairs, and since by the time formalist theory arrived on the scene of criticism literature was already what was mirrored in the structure of interpretation (in its totality, what is mirrored in the structure of literary interpretation as a universe of discourse), the fact that formalism attempted an explanation in metaphysical terms, in terms themselves vulnerable to attacks like Derrida's, is now only of historical interest.

Let us imagine, for instance, an absurdly oversimplified moment in the history of science, a moment in the seventeenth century, say, in which physics is universally taken to explain or elucidate the visible presence of God in nature. And let us further imagine a physicist, a severe rationalist or a temperamental scholastic, who accepts as the sole basis of his faith the ontological proof. Let us now supply our physicist with a friend, a skeptic of Hobbesian inclinations who is also a gifted logician, who undertakes to demonstrate to the physicist that the ontological proof is inadequate or mistaken in its own terms. The conversation begins after supper, and by the early hours of the morning the ontological proof has been, for the physicist, demolished: there is, he confesses wearily, no valid inference from the thought of something to the conclusion that that something must exist.

The point is that the demolition of the ontological proof in this instance, and with it the physicist's notion of physics as an elucidation of God's visible presence in nature, in no way touches the essential relation between physics as a universe of discourse and the state of affairs projected by physics as an object of inquiry: the physicist, if after this disheartening episode he is still prone to look about for another theory of what he does *as* a physicist, is simply left to discover another explanation or justification of his field of inquiry. And, just as important, he will not be liable in the light of his disenchantment to mistake the phenomenal world projected by physics for the ordinary world: where the ordinary man sees a table or a tree, physics will continue to see a colorless dance of whirling particles.

To see all this as a parable of contemporary theory, or at least of theoretical controversy, is to see that Derrida and his disciples correspond to the skeptical friend of the beleaguered physicist, his assault on the metaphysics of presence to the skeptic's assault on the ontological proof, and that the results are the same. An assault on the theory of literary autonomy, even a complete demolition of its metaphysical claims, leaves untouched what the theory attempts to account for, the existence of literature as a phenomenal reality projected by objective interpretation, a literary universe composed of literary worlds.

The great value of Derrida's theory of interpretation is that it exposes the inadequacy, the crudeness or vagueness or ill-thought-outedness, of a concept indispensable to inquiries into literary meaning. If we are unable to say what we mean by the concept of a literary world when its temporary alliance with the theory of autonomy has been dissolved, and if we yet see that the phenomenal reality to which the term "world" refers is as much a reality as ever, as much as ever the state of affairs that constitutes the object of inquiry, the immediate problem is to work out terms adequate to a pursuit of literary knowledge. And, at the same time, to search out that inadequacy of previous explanation or justification which throws light on our present confusion.

The source of confusion is suggested almost parenthetically in Derrida's description of "une scène d'écriture dans une scène d'écriture." If we omit the phrase that immediately follows ("et ainsi sans fin"), which is meant to justify a mode of interpretation leading to a free and infinite play of signification, we encounter a new notion of the text as embodying a literary world. For what Derrida unconscious-

22

ly raises (unconsciously, because his argument is directed toward quite another end) is the possibility that what we normally call the world of the literary work in reality contains a plurality of worlds not identical with itself. It is this possibility that the vast and labyrinthine structure of the *Life of Johnson* powerfully invites us to consider.

To see deconstructivist theory simply as the spearhead of a hostile metaphysics, that is to say, is to miss altogether what it may tell us about certain weaknesses in our own mode of interpretation. Is not our attempt to explain the structure of the *Life* through its resemblance to other literary models (for example, to the *Odyssey* or *Tom Jones* or the comedy of manners) simply a special instance of what Barthes describes as the search for "a model transcendent to several texts (and thus, all the more so of a model transcendent to all texts)"? When we abandon that search, begin instead to gaze into the *Life* at that plurality of worlds we glimpse from this new perspective, we are doing precisely what Barthes has in mind when he asks us to consider the text as its own model.

Our enterprise would not appear in this light to Barthes himself, as caught up in the possibilities of free play and infinite signification as Derrida, but that is of no real moment: it is what the deconstructivist concept of the text tells us about our own concepts that offers the promise of theoretical synthesis, of a new perspective and a new interpretive vocabulary to meet the demands of problems as otherwise puzzling as the structure of the *Life of Johnson*. If what we normally call the world of the *Life* indeed contains a plurality of worlds, we are invited to leave behind any conflict or quarrel between deconstructivist theory and objective interpretation and seek instead to explain on just what terms this could be so.

To argue that what we normally call the world of the *Life of Johnson* contains other worlds is to put enormous pressure on a conventional understanding of the concept of a literary world. For what one means by "world" is precisely a sphere of literary reality within which all elements exist in a coherent relation to one another. To introduce as even one of these elements a world coherent in itself, incompatible with or perhaps even antagonistic to the world of the work as a whole, seems fatally to undermine what one meant by world in the first instance. Does not that world, previously coherent as a configuration of subordinate elements, under this new pressure shiver and fragment, until one is left with nothing one should want to call a literary world?

Yet the dilemma is not a real one, for what we encounter here is a new concept of what constitutes a literary world, a more complex and precise perspective on what we formerly tried to explain in terms less satisfactory to our purposes. For what is under scrutiny in all this is not the concept of literary worlds, but what we have understood to belong to that concept. To argue that what I normally mean by the world of the *Life* contains other worlds implies only that what I have normally meant mistakes things in some essential way, that the *Life*, instead of existing as one world within which others are contained, may instead be seen as a coherent system or network of worlds in relation to each other.

As I shall pursue the implications of this concept through the remainder of the present study, the most immediate concern is how such a perspective translates into interpretive method. For if my usual notion of a literary world should turn out to be a metaphor after all, am I not in danger of merely substituting one metaphor for another? To argue that a notion of the *Life* as a world containing a plurality of worlds bears the traces of an inadequate interpretive vocabulary, that we understand its narrative and thematic structure only when this gives way to a notion of the *Life* as a system of separate worlds in relation to one another, is unavoidably to suggest a new or at least much refined mode of interpretation; the superiority of any new perspective, if it is indeed superior to the old, must consist at least in this.

If we consider for a moment the ways in which the usual perspective on the *Life* is inadequate to give an account of its structure, however, we may see almost immediately the potential superiority of the alternative I have barely sketched. For present purposes, perhaps, a single example may suffice: whatever we normally mean by the world of a literary work, it is at least obvious that in dealing with narrative we closely associate the concept with an idea of narrative consciousness, of the narrator as a mediating presence between us and the world of the story. This is in fact just what we have in mind when we recognize a certain affinity between the *Life* and a novel like *Tom Jones*. As the narrator of *Tom Jones* mediates between us and the world inhabited by Tom and Sophy and Squire Western, we want to say, Boswell as narrator mediates between us and the world inhabited by Johnson, Burke, Goldsmith, and the rest of the huge cast of characters who populate the *Life*.

It is purely a matter of convenience, however, to say that our usual model of narrative posits the narrator as a mediating presence or consciousness between the world of the story and us—that is, any actual audience of actual readers. What is important to our concerns is that the model may be translated into spatial terms: here, at some point outside the story, is the audience (whether an actual audience or an imaginary audience posited by the work itself does not much matter at this point). There, as it were on the other side of the narrator's consciousness, lies the world of the story. And in the space between, organizing and guiding and giving shape to our perception of that world, is the mediating voice of the narrator.

Yet to translate the model into spatial terms is evidently to do it less than full justice, for what is missing from the account is a principle of total coherence implied by our notion of narrative consciousness. As my world *is* the world of my consciousness, in just the same sense as I cannot at this moment perceive visually anything that lies outside my visual field, the narrator's consciousness in relation to the world of the story is enclosing and all-embracing, a medium within which the events we call the story emerge and take on a separate existence of their own. Thus we are led to identify the coherence of the world of the narrative with the coherence of the narrator's consciousness of that world.

None of this is in the least satisfactory, of course—that is partly the point—but it is at least clear that I am invoking something like this model when I envision the *Life of Johnson* as embodying a coherent world. For how else am I to account for Boswell's perspective as narrator, the only perspective in the work that, so to speak, stands outside the world inhabited by Johnson and views it as a whole? Thus, whenever we are aware of Boswell as a mediating presence or consciousness, our sense of narrative structure tends to suggest a familiar explanation of how things stand in the world of the *Life*:

> He received me very courteously; but, it must be confessed, that his apartment, and furniture, and morning dress, were sufficiently uncouth. His brown suit of cloaths looked very rusty; he had on a little old shrivelled unpowdered wig, which was too small for his head; his shirt-neck and knees of his breeches were loose; his black worsted stockings ill drawn up; and he had a pair of unbuckled shoes by way of slippers. But all these slovenly particularities were forgotten the moment that he began to talk. (I.396)[8]

This is Boswell paying his first visit to Johnson in his chambers at the Temple, a few days after their famous

[8] All parenthetical references to the *Life of Johnson* are to the Hill-Powell edition: *The Life of Johnson*, ed. G. B. Hill, rev. L. F. Powell, 6 vols. (Oxford: Oxford University Press, 1934-1964).

meeting at Davies's bookshop. And as the elements of Boswell's account of Johnson at home come into focus, it seems obvious that our usual model of narrative structure serves very well to explain what is going on: here is Boswell, a narrator whose consciousness of events has controlled our perception since the opening pages of the *Life*, moving inward toward the center of Johnson's world (or, alternatively, an older Boswell gazing back in retrospect on an earlier self who has penetrated Johnson's private domain). Without some notion of mediating perspective we should be altogether at a loss: there is no Johnson apart from this slovenly figure in shriveled wig and unbuckled shoes, only a blankness on the page.

When we dwell in this manner on what we are seeing and how we are seeing it, we are in turn drawn to explain the world of the *Life*, the world at this moment inhabited by Johnson in loose breeches and rusty clothes, almost wholly in terms of Boswell's perception of things. At just this moment, for instance, we understand that the structure of Boswell's own perception is being determined by a troubled tension between an abstract and idealized Johnson whose voice he has heard in the *Rambler* and *Rasselas*, and the uncouth figure who stands before him now: "I had for several years read his works with delight and instruction, and had the highest reverence for their authour, which had grown up in my fancy into a kind of mysterious veneration, by figuring to myself a state of solemn elevated abstraction, in which I supposed him to live in the immense metropolis of London" (I.383-84).

Though it will return to trouble Boswell's perception of Johnson throughout the *Life*, the tension is momentarily resolved at the instant Johnson begins to speak: "but all these slovenly particularities were forgotten the moment he began to talk." And in its resolution we see the world of the *Life* as a whole taking shape: on the one hand there will always be this slovenly and uncouth Johnson, a Johnson given to unaccountable eccentricities and ludicrous gesticulations, to behavior always odd and sometimes disgusting, unimaginable as a moral hero or a great man. On the other there will always be the Johnson who comes into existence at the moment of speech, a Johnson whose smallest talk opens up a luminous world of mind and wit and intellectual passion, a figure inconceivable except in terms of greatness.

At any such moment, it is the power of mind or language to annihilate the world of physical appearances that accounts for the resolution. It is not that the luminosity of Johnson's conversation creates an illusion that causes one to forget or ignore the slovenly particularities of his appearance and surroundings, but that in the moment of his speech one suddenly sees that it was physical reality itself, a reality of shriveled wigs and unbuckled shoes, that was the illusion. One remembers what one had forgot, and what can be recalled only in extraordinary circumstances—and Johnson talking is, throughout the *Life*, the most extraordinary of circumstances—that our heart's being and home is with infinitude, that there is only the world of mind.

Yet we want, at the moment Johnson opens the door of his chambers in the Temple, to explain all this in terms of Boswell's consciousness or perception of Johnson in his world. And the *Life* powerfully invites us to see things in just this way: it was through reading Johnson's works, after all, seeing in his writings a luminous revelation of mind in language, that Boswell formed a mysterious veneration for the abstract and idealized Johnson whom he imagines as living in a state of solemn elevated abstraction in London. This is precisely the Johnson, no longer abstract or idealized but real and present, who comes into being at the moment of speech, speech being no less than writing a revelation of mind in language. It is as though Boswell, beginning from a true perception of things and passing temporarily through an illusion of physical appearances, has returned to the greater reality he knew before.

When our sense of Boswell as a mediating presence is as

strong as this, we have no difficulty in explaining events or episodes within the story that seem to follow the same pattern. Thus the story of Hogarth's first encounter with Johnson at the house of Richardson the novelist:

> While he was talking, he perceived a person standing at a window in the room, shaking his head, and rolling himself about in a strange ridiculous manner. He concluded that he was an ideot, whom his relations had put under the care of Mr. Richardson, as a very good man. To his great surprize, however, this figure stalked forwards to where he and Mr. Richardson were sitting, and all at once took up the argument, and burst out into an invective against George the Second. . . . In short, he displayed such a power of eloquence, that Hogarth looked at him with astonishment, and actually imagined that this ideot had been at the moment inspired. (I.146-47)

The explanation of the scene, one wants to say, lies in its proportion of external appearances to speech. It is the tyranny of physical appearances, the overpowering image of Johnson shaking his head and rolling himself about, that cannot be wholly annihilated by his sudden burst of eloquence. Had the speech led to conversation, to what Johnson himself sometimes calls exchange of mind, the illusion would inevitably have been dispelled and Hogarth would have seen the reality that Boswell sees, that all who come to know Johnson at all well see, that we see ourselves throughout the *Life*. When Johnson falls back into silence, however, all that can happen does happen, and Hogarth is left to imagine that he has seen an idiot inspired.

When Johnson's speech is allowed to dominate the scene, on the other hand, we have within the world of the story events or episodes that exactly correspond to Boswell's own perception of Johnson. Thus Langton's first meeting with Johnson may be seen as a miniature version of Boswell's own visit to the Temple chambers: "Mr. Langton was exceedingly surprised when the sage first appeared. . . . From perusing his writings, he fancied he should see a decent, well-drest, in short, a remarkably decorous philosopher. Instead of which, down from his bed-chamber, about noon, came, as newly risen, a huge uncouth figure, with a little dark wig which scarcely covered his head, and his clothes hanging loose about him. But his conversation was so rich, so animated, and so forcible . . . that he conceived for him that veneration and attachment which he ever preserved" (I.247-48). And so Langton, as Boswell comes to do ten years later, penetrates to the center of Johnson's private world.

None of this seems to threaten a sense of Boswell as a mediating presence, as a narrator whose all-embracing consciousness explains the coherence we see and wish to explain. The Hogarth episode means what it means, after all, precisely because it works against the primary reality established by Boswell's perception of things, and in Langton's meeting with Johnson we are dealing not with Langton's consciousness of Johnson but with Boswell's consciousness of that consciousness. It is through Langton that we see Johnson as a huge uncouth figure newly risen from bed, but through Boswell, gazing at the episode from outside its boundaries in time and space, that we see Langton appearing at the door.

The great problem with this sort of explanation of the structure of the *Life* is that, even as it serves to elucidate much, it leaves so much out of account. For the *Life* is a narrative in which, for anything from brief moments to vast stretches of time, Boswell's mediating consciousness is in a manner of speaking suspended, giving us something like a direct or unmediated glimpse of the world on the other side. And whenever we gaze into this world, we have an overpowering sense that things are not altogether as Boswell sees them, that there is a different and often a more disturbing reality to be accounted for. Throughout the *Life*, for instance, Boswell includes in the text passages from Johnson's *Prayers and Meditations*, and in them we always encounter some version of the same reality:

'My thoughts have been clouded with sensuality; and, except that from the beginning of this year I have, in some measure, forborne excess of strong drink, my appetites have predominated over my reason. A kind of strange oblivion has overspread me, so that I know not what has become of the last year; and perceive that incidents and intelligence pass over me, without leaving any impression.' (I.482)

'Since the last Easter I have reformed no evil habit, my time has been unprofitably spent, and seems as a dream that has left nothing behind. *My memory grows confused, and I know not how the days pass over me.* Good Lord deliver me.' (I.487)

The world revealed in the *Prayers and Meditations*, a private world of terror and spiritual anguish, of gloom and misery and despair, must be taken by our usual mode of interpretation as a world-within-a-world, a dark and disquieting realm of suffering that we occasionally glimpse as lying behind the outward conviviality of the conversation scenes.[9] Yet this is precisely to deny that world its reality, to insist that the only actuality is Johnson, all wit and energy and animation, holding some company spellbound with the power of his eloquence. In relation to this sunlit scene of companionship and high spirits—the usual scene of Johnson's conversation in the *Life*—the bleak world of the *Prayers and Meditations* seems no more than a passing dream.

Yet the structure of the *Life* as a whole seems finally to deny this as a possibility, to demand that we gaze into the world revealed in the *Prayers and Meditations* as a reality to be taken on its own disturbing terms. And to do this is suddenly to experience a reversal of perspective that threatens utterly to annihilate that other world contained in Bos-

---

9 As I describe it in *The Boswellian Hero* (Athens, Ga.: Georgia University Press, 1979). I take this occasion to acknowledge the inadequacy of my argument there.

well's consciousness of events: " '*my time has been un-profitably spent, and seems as a dream that has left nothing behind.*' " For at such moments the dream, the shadow without substance, the world of ghostly insubstantiality, is nothing other than the outward world of the *Life* itself, the very sphere that exists in Boswell's perception as a solid and substantial world of food and drink, company and conversation, wit and argument and laughter.

The consequences of seeing the world revealed in the *Prayers and Meditations* in this way show in an immediate sense the limitations imposed by our usual model of narrative structure: it cannot be that both the private world of Johnson's anguish and the convivial outward world of the *Life* are dreams, shadowy and insubstantial in relation to some reality not yet glimpsed. It is that each is a dream in relation to the other, and when we have seen this we see that our mistake lay in identifying the world of the work with the world contained in Boswell's consciousness. Now that world, which we have viewed as embracing or enclosing everything within the biographical story, shrinks to become simply a world among others, and in some sense in antithetical relation to the gloomy world of Johnson's solitary suffering.

The notion of an antithetical relation as I am using it here must be redefined in terms of the structure I am attempting to explain. What it is meant to draw attention to is the sense in which that gloomy world revealed in the *Prayers and Meditations* is alien to and threatens the outward world of the *Life,* the sense in which it, as it were, refuses to be contained by Boswell's perspective—or, indeed, by the perspective of everyone in the *Life* who gazes uneasily into its depths and turns a troubled glance away. If one means for a moment by the world of the *Life* the total gaze of Johnson's world as it contemplates his anguish, one understands in a moment why that realm of private suffering remains beyond the reach of other perceptions; humankind, as T. S. Eliot said, cannot bear very much reality, and a reality like this remains in some sense forever alien.

Yet the tendency to see the realm of the *Prayers and Meditations* as somehow contained within the larger world identified with Boswell's consciousness as narrator is not altogether due to a limited or inadequate model of narrative structure. For on one level, Boswell, like other inhabitants of Johnson's world, does try to accommodate the troubling reality of Johnson's inward suffering, to make a place for it in his scheme of things. Thus the usual tone of his comments on the *Prayers and Meditations*: "The pious gratitude with which he acknowledges mercies upon every occasion is very edifying; as is the humble submission which he breathes, when it is the will of his heavenly Father to try him with afflictions" (I.305).

At such moments we are dealing not with genuine accommodation but with denial and domestication: the terrible reality of Johnson's anguish becomes a matter of edification, and Johnson himself is transformed into a comfortable paragon of wholly conventional piety. To say that the world contained in Boswell's consciousness is simply one of the worlds of the *Life*, or that it exists in antithetical relation to other worlds, is simultaneously to recognize that this sort of thing is going on continuously throughout his portion of the biographical story, that the Johnson who exists within his perception is a Johnson constructed to meet the demands of his own spiritual anxiety, a reassuring creation of his own troubled spirit.

Though we perceive all this most clearly when considering Boswell's perception as narrator, largely because the world contained in his consciousness is so prominent among the other worlds of the *Life*, it represents something like a universal phenomenon. For the *Life* gives us a world composed of worlds in which everyone gazes inward toward Johnson, and in which everyone creates or constructs a more comfortable Johnson who can be accommodated within an ordinary scheme of things. And always, in Johnson's speech or letters or the *Prayers and Meditations*, we glimpse another Johnson who refuses all accommodation, who escapes the limits of ordinary perception and bursts the bonds of any familiar scheme.

In the relation between the world of Boswell's consciousness and the private world of the *Prayers and Meditations*, then, I have isolated only one axis in that vast network of antithetical relations that is the structure of the *Life of Johnson*. To see that the world of the *Prayers and Meditations* exists in relation to Boswell's perception as an antiworld, a world alien and threatening and forever resisting attempts to contain it within the boundaries of a consciousness more ordinary than its own extraordinary reality, is simultaneously to grasp the relation of every world of the *Life* to every other, and to glimpse in the relation of world to antiworld a principle that elucidates the structure of the *Life* as a whole.

STRUCTURE AND STRUCTURALITY

To SEE the structure of the *Life of Johnson* as a structure of antithetical relations is not only to abandon the search for a model transcendent to several or all texts, but at the same time to dwell on what Derrida has called "la structuralité de la structure," to explore the possibilities that emerge when we begin to think of the text as its own model. Our dismay when we come to confront the structure of the *Life*, our sense of bewilderment and uncertainty, is surely a consequence of our having, in deconstructivist terms, posited a false or arbitrary center of coherence. Yet since we can go a great way toward explaining the structure of the *Life* by doing this, it is obvious that the procedure was not altogether false; it is simply that, after a certain point, we seem always to arrive at one or another impasse.

To conceive of the *Life* as being its own model, then, is to pursue one of the central insights of deconstructivist theory, to recognize as a possibility of structure "the co-presence in literary works (broadly speaking) of mixed or even discontinuous orders of discourse."[1] I translate the insight into objective terms when I add that interpretation may view such orders of discourse as embodying worlds of perception or consciousness, but the point about the structure of the *Life* will then be analogous: what confuses or bewilders us about that structure is that the *Life* seems constantly to be asserting norms that it then threatens or undermines or subverts, so that the search for a single principle of inner coherence is continuously frustrated. The confusion ends when we see that this is itself a prin-

---

[1] Geoffrey Hartman, "Literary Criticism and Its Discontents," *Critical Inquiry*, 3 (Winter 1976), 218.

ciple of coherence, that the way the *Life* questions or quali-
fies its own norms explains its structure as narrative.

Throughout the *Life*, for instance, we hear Boswell wor-
rying anxiously about the form of his narrative, defending
his biographical method against an imaginary horde of
scoffers or detractors, hovering anxiously above the text
and considering it *as* a text. Though a conventional vocabulary of interpretation leads us to identify this as a pattern
of narrative self-consciousness, and though the pattern is
insistent enough to represent what is normally called a
theme, something makes us resist explaining the pattern
as anything like a "theme of self-consciousness" in the *Life
of Johnson*. And properly so, for though the pattern is
significant to an understanding of the thematic structure
of the *Life*, what it really shows is Boswell's uneasy awareness that his work is continuously subverting its own norms.

This anxiety about form or structure, about the status
of the text as a text, shows itself in the opening pages of
the *Life*. "I profess to write," says Boswell, "not his panegyrick, which must be all praise, but his Life": "in every picture there should be shade as well as light, and when I de-
lineate him without reserve, I do what he himself recom-
mended, both by his precept and his example" (I.30). And
Boswell then immediately quotes, by way of precept, Johnson's own remarks on biography in *Rambler* 60: "There are
many who think it an act of piety to hide the faults or
failings of their friends, even when they can no longer
suffer by their detection; we therefore see whole ranks of
characters adorned with uniform panegyrick, and not to be
known from one another but by extrinsick and casual circumstances."

On one level, all that is occurring here is that Boswell is
warning his audience about a greater complexity of structure than that to which they are accustomed in biographical
narrative. The norm of the classical encomium, or of such
modern examples as Walton's *Lives*, is unreserved praise,
what Johnson calls uniform panegyric. The *Life*, Boswell

is in effect announcing, will observe this norm—"to be as he was, is indeed subject of panegyrick enough to any man in this state of being"—but then it will also include elements that seem to subvert the norm, to reveal a Johnson who is an object, if not of blame or dispraise, of something not entirely compatible with praise. The text will, in a word, both incorporate and reject the panegyric model.

Yet on a deeper level, and in a number of simultaneous ways, what we see here is the text calling attention to its own antithetical structure. There is, first of all, the ambiguity of Boswell's metaphor: "in every picture there should be shade as well as light." At first glance the metaphor seems perfectly suited to the *Life* as a literary form: light and shade in painting are neutral compositional elements, and surely we can imagine them as having their counterparts in literary composition. In this context, however, it is obvious that the metaphor carries not merely a compositional but a moral burden; as we speak of dark intentions or designs, black thoughts—even, in modern slang, of shady characters—the shade in Johnson's story suggests some world lying beyond the sunlit moral borders of panegyric.

To recognize the ambiguity is simultaneously to recognize that Boswell's metaphor is really a metaphor about structure. The existence within the *Life* of a world or worlds that lie outside the moral sunshine of uniform panegyric argues an essential discontinuity that no appeal to transcendent models can disguise: panegyric that blames or dispraises is no longer panegyric, but neither is it not panegyric, for it is only through the breakdown or violation of the norm of formal praise that we understand what has broken down or been violated. The *Life* does not blame Johnson, nor, strictly speaking, does it dispraise him, but it does continuously introduce elements that exist in antithetical relation to the norms of panegyric.

This is the least significant aspect of Boswell's anxious remarks, however. Much more significant is the manner in which this portion of the work enacts the puzzle of its own discontinuities. It is not merely that Boswell's metaphor shows the text calling attention to its own antithetical structure, but that the sudden juxtaposition of Boswell's remarks with Johnson's magisterial comments on biography displays the very antitheticality to which the metaphor is calling attention. In that expanded interpretive vocabulary suggested by deconstructivist theory, one may say that these two passages stand in relation to each other as world to antiworld.

When we begin by recognizing that Boswell's remarks on the form of the *Life* belong to the world that we identify with his mediating consciousness as biographical narrator (even as they momentarily transcend that world to contemplate the text as text), we acknowledge that the introduction into the text of a passage from Johnson's writings represents a suspension of narrative consciousness, a glimpse into a world not identical with the world contained in or implied by Boswell's own perception of things. That world, so far, need not exist in antithetical relation to the world of Boswell's consciousness, but it is at least recognizable as a world.

Throughout the *Life*, whenever Johnson's writings are quoted, any single passage implies the existence of a total and coherent sphere of moral thought implicitly identified with the whole body of Johnson's writings. As a single sentence in a language may be said to imply the total structure of the language to which it belongs—for the same system of rules that generated this sentence may generate every other in the language—this passage from *Rambler* 60 may be said to imply the existence of a world of mind only partially or incompletely represented by *Rasselas* or *The Lives of the Poets* or, indeed, by *The Rambler* itself. When Boswell's narrative consciousness is momentarily suspended, it is thus as though the *Life* had brought into itself an element of a world not its own.

Yet the total body of an author's writings need not be considered as embodying a world, even though we are accustomed to speaking of the world of Dickens or the world of Chaucer, or to say that what occurs in the world of Hardy would be unimaginable in the Dickens world. What invites one to speak of world and antiworld in this instance is that the *Life* as a whole always demands that one envision Johnson's writings in this manner, that behind every quoted or extracted passage lies an unquoted totality that represents an invisible and magisterial source of authority for the image of Johnson given us in the narrative itself. Without that authority, existing unseen behind every portrayal of Johnson in speech or action, the structure of the narrative would collapse.

This does not give us an antiworld, however, or in this case a world existing in antithetical relation to Boswell's perception of things. Yet as we have seen, the antithetical relation is there: it is what Boswell recognizes when, having known Johnson only through his writings and entertaining a mysterious veneration for an imaginary philosopher living in a state of solemn elevated abstraction, the door of Johnson's Temple chambers opens to reveal a slovenly figure in unbuckled shoes and shriveled wig. It is what Langton recognizes when, having formed in his mind from a reading of Johnson's works the image of a "remarkably decorous philosopher," he enters the door to discover a huge uncouth figure newly risen from bed.

When one undertakes to elucidate all this in terms of antithetical structure, a crucial point is in danger of getting lost: Boswell's imaginary philosopher, living in the state of solemn abstraction that accords with the elevated wisdom of his writings, Langton's remarkably decorous philosopher, the exalted and magisterial presence envisioned by all those who know Johnson solely through his works—all these are real, converging on a single projection necessary to complete the idea of Johnson's writings as a complete

and coherent world. It is only the relation of this abstract
and idealized Johnson to the uncouth figure who confronts
Boswell or Langton that demands explanation in terms of
antithesis; in relation to the world of his writings, the
Johnson they imagine to exist exists.

When we conceive of the world embodied in Johnson's
writings as an antiworld, we suddenly glimpse an explanation of the sort of puzzle with which the structure of the
Life is continually confronting us. The shade in Boswell's
biographical portrait will be composed of everything antithetical to an image of Johnson as an idealized philosopher and sage—his roughness, his eccentricity, his shriveled
wigs and unbuckled shoes. And in defense of his perception
of that rough and slovenly and uncouth Johnson, Boswell
introduces, as an outside authority testifying in his favor,
the magisterial Johnson of the writings: it is the remarkably decorous philosopher, the sage living and writing in a
state of solemn elevated abstraction, who is summoned to
defend the portrait of the uncouth creature who appears
at the door of the Temple chambers.

Yet it is not quite right to say that Boswell introduces
the idealized sage and moralist here, though that is what
one normally says when a narrator quotes an outside authority. What we are really seeing is one of the possibilities
of antithetical structure, something explained only when
we see that the *Life* posits the world of Johnson's writings
and the world of Boswell's perception as complete and coherent in themselves, and the relation of each to the other
as of world to antiworld. For this sort of juxtaposition
occurs throughout the *Life*, and is perhaps the most prominent feature of its structure; in every sudden transition
from narrative to conversation scene, from firsthand narration to secondhand account, from text to letter, we encounter the same sort of puzzle, and always we are invited
to see what is occurring in terms of antithetical structure.

In speaking of world and antiworld within the *Life*,
however, I am speaking really of two different things. To

speak of an antiworld is in one sense not to speak of anything one should want to describe as a literary world, but of the network of antithetical relations of which the structure of the *Life* is composed, of the antithetical relation of world to world within the text. When I speak of Boswell's perception of events or Johnson's writings as separate worlds, on the other hand, I am focusing on something that the normal use of "world" makes wholly familiar: the completeness and coherence of the sphere of literary reality identified by the term, and the fact that it seems to have a distinct phenomenological horizon or circumference.

This is why, for instance, the sudden transitions or juxtapositions that according to our usual model of narrative structure make the form of the *Life* so anomalous are readily explained in terms of world and antiworld. And this is true even when the text disguises its own discontinuities, for in one sense every such transition in the *Life* is wholly discontinuous. Let us consider one last time exactly what is occurring when Boswell quotes from *Rambler* 60 in defense of his own conception of biography. Is he not doing something formally identical to what he does when, a page or so later, he quotes for the same purposes, in the original Greek and in translation, the thoughts of Plutarch on biographical form and method?

If the problem demands scrutiny, it is because our usual model of narrative structure suggests that there is no problem at all. A narrator who quotes from a work external to his narrative is not, we want to say, doing anything essentially anomalous or discontinuous: the passage quoted simply becomes a feature of the narrative itself. Yet even in the most conventional instance of such citation or extraction we can see a certain suggestion of antithetical structure. If the passage Boswell quotes had been all that Plutarch wrote, or all that survived of what he wrote, there would be no problem. It is not. Behind the passage lies the entire world of Plutarch's *Lives*—Boswell describes him as "the prince of ancient biographers"—and that is the entire point: what the passage is meant to assert is precisely a relation between the separate worlds of Plutarchan and Boswellian biography.

In formal or structural terms, the same sort of thing occurs when Boswell quotes *Rambler* 60 in his own defense. What gives the moment its complexity is that this summons one conception of Johnson in defense of another conception of Johnson, but this can occur only because it is, so to speak, written into the possibilities of antithetical structure from the outset. The discontinuity is only superficially disguised by Boswell's hopeful remarks about his own biographical method following Johnson's precept, for these remarks too belong to the world of his perception or narrative consciousness, a world not identical with the separate world of Johnson's writings.

In one sense, then, a conception of the *Life* as a structure of antitheses does begin by seeing that it shivers or fragments into separate worlds—or rather, not that but how it does so. The most obvious instance is the sudden blankness of the page whenever there is an abrupt and unexplained transition from, say, narration to correspondence (and the *Life* does this so often that anyone considering its structure will have a repeated sense of anomaly). Yet the same sort of thing is only slightly less obvious when there is a vestige of conventional transition, as when a single sentence ("On the 21st of March, I was happy to find myself again in my friend's study") plunges us into a conversation scene cast in the form of dramatic dialogue.

This is in fact Boswell's usual mode of treating one sort of conversation scene, the scene that typically takes place when he first meets Johnson after having made the long journey down from Edinburgh. And in conventional terms one can explain well enough what is going on: the single sentence that announces that Boswell has once again materialized at Johnson's door in effect collapses the separation, geographical and cultural, of the worlds of Edinburgh and London, reminds us that the center of the narrative is Johnson and his conversation. Yet what we see in such terms as these is made possible only by a deeper antithesis of structure, the antithesis between the world of Boswell's consciousness and the world of unmediated speech that is embodied in the conversation scenes.

Yet it now becomes obvious that we can no longer continue to leave unscrutinized the notion of mediation in such contexts as this. It is clear enough that the notion in some way defines our usual model of narrative structure, and that I must invoke it too to describe an alternative model of antithetical structure; what is not clear at all is what exactly we mean (or are trying to mean) by the term. What does it mean, after all, to describe Boswell as a mediating presence or consciousness between us and the world inhabited by Johnson and his circle of acquaintance? Or to say that Johnson's speech in the *Life*, as representing a suspension of Boswell's mediating consciousness, gives us an unmediated glimpse of that world?

At the same time, it is perhaps equally obvious that I shall not arrive at an adequate account of mediation until I have at least a provisional account of antithetical structure, for this structure is just what one begins to see in any transition from world to antiworld. Let us assume for the moment, then, that the structure of the *Life* can be seen in some such perspective as is suggested by the Saussurean or structuralist model of language as a system of differences without positive terms. The relation of world to antiworld, and the otherwise puzzling notion that a world can also, as a consequence of antithetical structure, be seen as an antiworld, may be accounted for in terms of such a system of differences.

The Saussurean model may in one sense be described as an attempt to get us past an illusion—namely, the illusion that any term in a system is positive by virtue of reference to something outside the system. Thus, to borrow almost in its entirety Jonathan Culler's fine example, our use of any such color-term as brown invites us to think of

43

a relation between the concept of brown and objects existing, as we say, in a world independent of language. (There are tremendous philosophical problems, as Wittgenstein showed, with this use of the phrase "concept of brown," but they need not impede me here.) The shoes I am wearing today are brown, and so is my pipe and my tweed jacket, and there is a powerful suggestion that these facts somehow play a role in determining the meaning of "brown."

Yet we come to see that the referentiality of the term brown—or, let us say rather, the fact that it may be *used* to refer to objects independent of the system of language— gives no adequate account of its meaning; indeed, no adequate account of anything we should want on a more general level to call meaning. Suppose, for instance (I am still following Culler) that we had as a guest a being from some planet on which everything was colorless. To ease the shock of acculturation we whisk him or her or it under cover of total darkness from spaceship to blank room. Then, next morning, we undertake to teach him the meaning or concept of brown. How should we proceed?

The point of the Saussurean model is that it will be useless to bring our guest my pipe, my shoes, my tweed jacket, and then an indefinite succession of brown objects. It is only when we set a red object alongside a brown object, using the terms red and brown to explain the difference on which their meaning depends, that our extraterrestrial friend begins to grasp their meaning. And so with the blue and orange objects we bring in next: our guest is learning with the help of objects, but *what* he is learning is a system in which "red" has meaning only in its relation to and difference from "orange," "blue," "brown," and the rest.

When we conceive of an analogous model of narrative structure, referentiality is no longer a problem: we have never wanted to say that *Hamlet* or *Paradise Lost* are descriptions of some actuality independent of themselves, that they refer to the world in the way that the term brown refers to my shoes or my jacket. Yet the analogy contains a significant point for my purposes: when we describe the world of Boswell's consciousness in the *Life* as a world coherent and complete in itself, we are doing something very similar to what we do when we see "brown" as a positive term referring to shoes and jackets; we are endowing it with a substantiality, a positive claim to represent some sort of phenomenal reality, that is lacking in the antiworlds that define its existence.

What is illegitimate in linguistics may have great value in interpretation, that is to say, though it cannot even be said that the linguistic model escapes something of the same sort. We can, it is true, understand that "brown" signifies only as an element in a system of negative relations, that it is precisely what is *not* orange, blue, green, red, and so on. Yet when we so to speak gaze directly at the term brown and ponder its meaning, it does seem somehow more positive or substantial than the invisible system of unmentioned color terms that define its meaning. And when we go on to contemplate "red" the same sort of thing occurs: "brown" disappears to become part of the invisible system, and "red" occupies at least the foreground of contemplation.

In any event, something analogous to this quite legitimately occurs when we focus on antithetical structure in narrative, and it is related in an obvious way to our normal conception of a literary world. To say that Boswell's consciousness of things constitutes a world within the *Life of Johnson* is to invoke just the same explanatory model involved in speaking of the world of *Hamlet* or *Tom Jones*, to see it as having not only completeness and inner coherence but also the positive existence or substantiality that we attribute to any literary world. Further, I may so far explain what occurs within the world of Boswell's consciousness in the same terms as I explain what occurs within the worlds of *Hamlet* or *Tom Jones*.

Yet a model of antithetical structure at the same time demands, as our usual model of narrative structure does not, that we see the positive existence or substantiality of this world as an explanatory fiction, a momentary point of arrest in a movement toward total elucidation. For what gives this world its substantiality is the existence of a system of antiworlds possessing only a negative existence, a defining system of antitheses or differences that creates the momentary illusion of coherence and solidity. And these too demand explanation in their turn as positive or substantial worlds.

Explaining the narrative and thematic structure of the *Life* in terms of antithesis, then, involves moving through a system of defining differences in a way that·exposes the relations that explain the coherence of the system itself. In the moment that we speak of the scene revealed in the *Prayers and Meditations* as a world, it is the world of Boswell's narrative consciousness that dematerializes and takes its place in the invisible system of antithetical relations that define the positive and terrible reality of Johnson's private anguish (and now we see why, when the world of the *Prayers and Meditations* becomes a positive or primary reality, the rest of the *Life* appears "as a dream that has left nothing behind").

Though any such model of narrative structure seems to derive in some obvious way from deconstructivist theory, two of its features suggest that it is in reality only an expanded and refined version of a model we have long been accustomed to invoke. The first is that the notion of antithesis implied by the model is wholly neutral: it may be that the norms of one world within the system of antitheses are threatened or denied or undermined or subverted by the antiworlds that define its positive existence (and this occurs so frequently in the *Life* that it demands careful consideration), but this need not be so; the relation between world and antiworld may be as neutral—one wants to say benign—as that between blue and green.

46

The second feature of the expanded model that denies the metaphysical claims of deconstructivist theory is precisely that it posits an objective structure that can be explained in objective terms. To see the structure of the *Life* as a system of antitheses is in no way to license a mode of interpretation that aims at an utterly free play of signification, that begins by asserting and ends by having demonstrated its own autonomy. The structure of the *Life* exists as a puzzle precisely because it has so far resisted attempts at elucidation, exposed the inadequacy of primitive models of narrative structure by forcing us into this or that impasse. It is that which resisted our attempts before, a stable and objective structure, that yet remains to be explained.

This is the context in which one is led to ponder the notion of mediation as it defines both our usual model of narrative structure and an expanded model of antithetical structure. Again, what exactly are we trying to mean when we say that the narrator of *Tom Jones* mediates between us and the world inhabited by Tom and Sophy, or when we say, following the same model, that Boswell mediates between us and the world inhabited by Johnson and his circle? I may perhaps begin from one thing that is clear about such assertions, that their meaning depends not on any model of narrative structure but on some other model invoked to explain that structure.

Even to see as much as this is to suggest a direction for inquiry: the model invoked when I speak of mediation in narrative seems in some obvious way to be epistemological, a model of consciousness and perception. It is the analogy of consciousness that seems to lurk in the background, at least, whenever we identify the coherence of a narrative world with the narrator's mediating presence, for something like this coherence is assumed in every discussion of consciousness as a phenomenon; realism and idealism (including the extreme form of solipsism) depend on it equally, as does the method of phenomenology and even analytic philosophy.[2] "The world," wrote Wittgenstein in the *Tractatus*, "is *my* world."

In the same way, consciousness is present as an analogy whenever we attempt to account for the independence in narrative of what we call the world of the story. Though they are the objects of his contemplation, Tom and Sophy inhabit a different world from that of the narrator of *Tom Jones* precisely because their consciousnesses are separate from his, because their worlds are different from his world in just the same way as my world is different from yours. And this is true even of the inanimate world that we might otherwise suppose to lie in common among them, the fields and houses and roads of the story; part of what we mean by consciousness is that there can be no objects independent of some perception, and what things are depends on how they exist for consciousness. The fool, wrote Blake, sees not the same tree as the wise man sees.

The same sort of epistemological model seems to be involved whenever we attempt to explain plot or action. I want to say, for instance, that Tom and Sophy and Squire Western also exist as autonomous characters because they are volitional beings, because any action they will is as invisible to the narrator as any action I might take a minute or an hour from now is invisible to you at this instant. Yet even this reduces to the terms of an epistemological model: it is because my consciousness is opaque to you, because you cannot hear or see my thoughts, that this is so.

This is why what is usually called omniscient narration is not in any complete sense omniscient: if the narrator of *Tom Jones* possessed the omniscience of Calvin's God, and if in his charming and garrulous way he undertook to tell us what he knew, the possibility of what we call plot would simply disappear. It exists precisely because the narrator,

[2] Hume may be mentioned as an exception; yet even his famous "theater of the mind" metaphor assumes some principle of epistemological coherence.

along with his audience, in some sense has (or, in the case of retrospective narration, had) no way of knowing what a character will do next. The convention according to which an omniscient narrator reports the thoughts of characters applies only to their past consciousness, even if the past is only instantly past, and imitates not omniscience but the sort of inference we make when we perceive that our friend is in pain because he is wincing.

The problem of omniscient narration never arises in the *Life*, of course, because Boswell is a first-person narrator to whom the thoughts and motives of everyone else are opaque (except in the usual way that one infers them from outward behavior). Yet to see that even omniscient narration is less than omniscient is to see in clearer terms what the notion of mediation means when it is invoked to describe the structure of the *Life*: what we mean by mediation is something that corresponds to the epistemological model of consciousness of a conscious being, perception of someone whose pure perception of reality remains opaque.

The reason that we want to see the world revealed in the *Prayers and Meditations* as an unmediated vision of Johnson's inner experience, then, becomes clear. My consciousness of my own existence as a conscious being is the epistemological center of my world—it may be viewed, as by Husserl or Merleau-Ponty, as the essence of my being—and it is of some such consciousness as this that the *Prayers and Meditations* form a record: " 'My indolence, since my last reception of the sacrament, has sunk into grosser sluggishness, and my dissipation spread into wilder negligence. My thoughts have been clouded with sensuality; and . . . my appetites have predominated over my reason' " (I.482). For in addressing himself to his Creator Johnson is simultaneously speaking to himself about himself.

Yet no act of consciousness or perception may be viewed as wholly unmediated: to be aware of my own experience is to be aware of myself in the same way as I am at other times aware of others, and to be aware of *this* is to be conscious of my own consciousness of my existence as a conscious being; the self, Wittgenstein said, is not in the world but is a limit of the world. It is because the *Prayers and Meditations* correspond more nearly than anything else in the *Life* to the phenomenon of consciousness of one's own consciousness that they seem to provide an unmediated glimpse into the world of Johnson's private and solitary suffering.

For similar reasons, we want to see the conversation scenes of the *Life* as embodying an unmediated world of speech, and as existing somewhere in the middle distance between the private world of the *Prayers and Meditations* and the wholly mediated world of Boswell's narrative consciousness. For speech is in some sense the direct expression of consciousness, and through it we gaze into a world of thought and emotion that is otherwise opaque. This is why, whenever Johnson speaks directly in the *Life* (" 'Sir, a woman's preaching is like a dog's walking on its hinder legs. It is not done well; but you are surprized to find it done at all' ") we begin to construct a world independent of Boswell's consciousness of events.

It is the same epistemological model that leads us to see Boswell's narrative consciousness as existing at something like an outward extreme; what we want to describe in terms of mediation is his consciousness of Johnson as a conscious being—and a being, moreover, whose heroic and philosophic consciousness represents the central mystery of the *Life*. Thus Boswell, after an evening during which Johnson has several times burst into anger: "I compared him at this time to a warm West-Indian climate, where you have a bright sun, quick vegetation, luxuriant foliage, luscious fruits; but where the same heat sometimes produces thunder, lightening, and earthquakes, in a terrible degree" (III.300).

Our usual model of narrative structure serves well enough to explain what is occurring here: in describing Johnson in terms of cataclysmic natural forces, of thunder and earthquakes, Boswell is giving voice to just that sense of awe—of Johnson as something larger than life—that is shared by all those who inhabit his world.[3] Yet we must invoke something like an epistemological model to explain why he is compelled to search for similes at all: it is because the realm of inner thought and emotion that produced both Johnson's sparkling conversation and his angry outbursts remains wholly opaque both to us and to Boswell that it must be conjectured about, accommodated in some manner, described in figurative terms.

In the long conversation scene that precedes Boswell's meteorological simile, then, we contemplate the elements of narrative structure that the notion of mediation attempts to explain. At the furthest extreme, beyond either perception or description, lies the pure realm of Johnson's consciousness (and it is because the *Prayers and Meditations* come closest to revealing this realm that we see them as we do). Then, in the middle distance, there is Johnson's speech, at least the outward expression of that complex consciousness that can shift in an instant from brilliant wit to angry fulmination. Then, at the near extreme, there is Boswell, listening to Johnson's speech and through it conscious of his consciousness, whose description of events assert his mediating presence.

The great danger of invoking an epistemological model to explain what we mean by mediating perspective in narrative, however, is that we shall begin to see all this in epistemological terms (as do Poulet and other members of the Geneva School, for instance). Yet it should be clear that the model is only a model, that we are asserting only that what occurs in the *Life of Johnson* is in certain respects analogous to certain features of consciousness and perception. Neither Boswell nor Johnson is a conscious being in the sense that you and I are conscious beings—

[3] For a discussion of this scene in similar terms, see Felicity Nussbaum, "Boswell's Treatment of Johnson's Temper," *Studies in English Literature* (Summer 1974), pp. 421-33.

they are creatures of a world composed solely of words, and we use models and analogies only because in explaining the reality they inhabit we must borrow the terms of our explanation from the only world we know.

The relation between an antithetical model of narrative structure and the epistemological model we invoke in speaking of mediation is problematic, and I shall have occasion to examine it in some detail later in my inquiry. What seems important at the moment is the way each complements the other: if a conception of the *Life* as a structure of antithetical relations seems initially to fragment the *Life* into separate worlds—or, more properly, into a galaxy of relations among world and antiworld—it is so to speak along the lines of mediation that it fractures. It is precisely in epistemological terms that (to follow my earlier example) we see the relation of Boswell's narrative consciousness and the world revealed in the *Prayers and Meditations* as a relation between world and antiworld.

This is the context in which it becomes obvious that our usual model of narrative structure implies something significant about our broader notions of literary structure itself. For the model is what it is by virtue of existing at the midpoint on a continuum of structural possibilities, the extremes being represented by lyric poetry at one end and drama at the other. In lyric and drama (at least, our discussions of structure normally imply this) one discovers in pure or unmixed form those structural possibilities that narrative in various ways combines.[4] There are complications, of course, as when at the end of "Lycidas" we suddenly discover a speaker hitherto silent, or when at the

[4] "A lyric, like a drama, is a direct presentation, in which a single actor, the poet or his surrogate, sings, or muses, or speaks for us to hear or overhear. Add a second speaker, as Robert Frost does in 'The Death of the Hired Man' and we move toward drama. Let the speaker begin to tell of an event, as Frost does in 'The Vanishing Red,' and we move toward narrative." Robert Scholes and Robert Kellogg, *The Nature of Narrative* (Oxford: Oxford University Press, 1966), p. 4.

beginning of Shaw's plays a loquacious expositor lectures us on what we are about to read, but these are of interest precisely because they are violations of an ideal norm.

Our usual model of narrative structure seems, moreover, to begin at the lyric end of the continuum. For lyric structure seen in epistemological terms represents the world so absorbed into the consciousness of a single speaker that there is nothing remaining outside that consciousness: "Had we but world enough, and time / This coyness, lady, were no crime." The lady who exists as an internal or dramatic audience is here a vestigial reminder of a world unabsorbed by the speaker's consciousness, perhaps, but only that. She does not speak, and we feel her silent presence only as a final implication of his utterance. The rest, a world of worms and graves and deserts of vast eternity, dwells entirely within his mind and speech.

In narrative, with the emergence of a world of speech and action existing independent of the narrator's consciousness, we seem to be moving toward the extreme of drama. This is, for instance, what makes us want to say that the world of the story exists on the other side of the narrator's mediating consciousness. Yet what is significant here is that our usual model of narrative structure derives wholly from an idea of lyric form and ends in drama. We see the narrator as a mediating presence because the world of the story, if not altogether absorbed into his consciousness, is at least simultaneously present to his mind. Thus, for instance, the narrator of *Tom Jones* describing the virtuous Bridget Allworthy:

I have observed (tho' it may seem unaccountable to the reader) that this guard of prudence, like the trained bands, is always readiest to go on duty where there is the least danger. It often basely and cowardly deserts those paragons for whom the men are all wishing, sighing, dying, and spreading every net in their power; and constantly attends at the heels of that higher order of women, for whom the other sex have a more distant and awful respect, and whom (from despair, I suppose, of success) they never venture to attack.

The character of Miss Bridget herself, it is true, supplies the pretext for the narrator's tongue-in-cheek moralizing ("so discreet was she in her conduct, that her prudence was as much on the guard, as if she had had all the snares to apprehend which were ever laid for her whole sex"), and it is also true that Bridget will go on to play an important role in a story that we see as developing independent of his consciousness. Yet at such moments as this the narrator's mediating consciousness seems to enclose within itself the events of the story, to reduce them to the level of exempla for a broader and more complex perception of human moral and social nature. To ignore this, it seems, would amount to something like seeing Marvell's lyric not as a meditation on time and death but as an unadorned attempt at unprincipled seduction.

At the same time, it is the existence of a world independent of the narrator's consciousness that leads us to see narrative as existing at a midpoint on a continuum of structural possibilities; any scene in *Tom Jones* that gives us two characters speaking directly to each other simultaneously gives us an autonomous world of motive and speech and action. And the reason we see drama as existing at the other extreme of an abstract continuum is that it contains no suggestion of a mediating consciousness between us and the story, but simply a world in which autonomous beings address each other in direct terms. Again, there may be vestigial reminders of a mediating presence, as with stage directions or chorus or prologue, but these are interesting precisely as complications of an ideal possibility of structure.

There is, perhaps, nothing fatally misleading in this notion of a structural continuum, or even in the fact that interpretations of narrative seem always to give lyric a primary and drama only a marginal weight as models in descriptions of narrative form. Yet if the *Life of Johnson* powerfully invites us to explain its structure in terms of antithetical relations, it is clear that we shall have to revise radically our notion of where it exists on the continuum, even to the point of taking drama as a primary model of structure. This is the light, for instance, in which we might consider the dialogue of the conversation scenes:

WILKES. 'We have no City-Poet now: that is an office which has gone into disuse. The last was Elkanah Settle. There is something in *names* which one cannot help feeling. Now *Elkanah Settle* sounds so *queer,* who can expect much from that name? We should have no hesitation to give it for John Dryden, in preference to Elkanah Settle, from the names only, without knowing their different merits.' JOHNSON. 'I suppose, Sir, Settle did as well for Alderman in his time, as John Home could do now. Where did Beckford and Trecothick learn English?' (III.75-76)

This is the first Johnson-Wilkes encounter, perhaps the most famous conversation scene in the *Life.* The structure of the scene is complex—even, that is, when we do not consider its relation to the total structure of the *Life*—and to explain it we almost inevitably invoke both our usual model of narrative structure and the notion of an abstract continuum of structural possibilities. The scene begins, we want to say, in the world of Boswell's consciousness; when he has set in motion the machinery of the encounter, and long before either Johnson or Wilkes is aware that the other is going to be present at Dilly's dinner, the dramatic tension of the scene lies in Boswell's own sense of impending cataclysm or social eruption.

Then, as Johnson and Wilkes converge in the body on the scene of their encounter, as the episode begins to emerge as a reality independent of Boswell's consciousness, we move into another sphere. Beginning at the moment Wilkes overwhelms Johnson with polite attention, and continuing through a succession of neutral conversational topics to the moment when they join together in jokes against the Scotch, we have a scene that can be explained only in dramatic terms; this is what the casting of the scene into dramatic dialogue symbolizes, and this is what explains Boswell's disappearance as narrator and reappearance as a character within the scene.

When we invoke our usual model, that is, we have no choice but to say that Boswell's narrative consciousness has dwindled away to nothingness in the moment that Johnson and Wilkes are discussing Elkanah Settle, that it has been suspended or interrupted to give us an unmediated view of a separate reality. Yet though we can go far with this sort of explanation, there is always something it seems to leave out of account—or rather, something it seems to supply in violation of our actual sense of narrative structure. For to say that Boswell's consciousness as narrator has been suspended or interrupted is to assign the Wilkes scene a subordinate role within the structure of the *Life*, to say that it is somehow less real than the world contained in Boswell's perception of things.

The explanation suggested by an antithetical model of structure, on the other hand, reverses all this, sees the exchange between Wilkes and Johnson as enacting the major structural principle of the *Life* as a whole. For in dramatic dialogue, as in drama as a literary form, we discover a structure comprehensible only in terms of antithesis, a world in which speech signals a horizontal relation to conscious beings whose otherness is a condition of speech itself. Within such a world speech or language remains the primary means of mediation between mind and mind, but there is no longer any suggestion of the vertical perspective implied by the notion of a narrative consciousness hovering over the action as a whole.

56

If the *Life* invites us to see drama as the primary model of its structure, however, or at least to reverse our usual notion of an abstract continuum of structural possibilities and begin at the extreme represented by dramatic form, it is not simply because the conversation scenes are so primary a reality within the biographical story, or even because they are so often cast in purely dramatic form. For what occurs in the conversation scenes occurs whenever our usual model of narrative structure leads us to say that Boswell's narrative consciousness has been suspended or interrupted, whenever narration ceases and we encounter a letter or series of letters, a passage from Johnson's works or the *Prayers and Meditations*, or a second- or thirdhand account of his actions or speech.

Our usual model leads us to say something quite correct, then, when we explain that at the moment Johnson and Wilkes are discussing Elkanah Settle Boswell's mediating consciousness has dwindled to the point of nothingness. What it fails to do is deal with the total implication of this explanation, to go on and describe the *Life* as a world of antithetical relations in which Boswell as narrator, or, more precisely, the portions represented by his narration, simply play a major role. To explain the *Life* as an antithetical structure is to view Boswell in his role as narrator in somewhat the same way as we view the role of any important character in a drama.

All this does some violence to our usual notion of the narrator as a mediating presence, but its virtue is that it allows us to explain what otherwise frustrates our attempts at explanation. To view Boswell's narration in the *Life* not as a containing but as a distributed embodiment of his consciousness, much as we view Hamlet's or Lear's speeches in those plays, is to expose the network of antithetical relations that remains obscure when we assume him, even when wholly silent, to be hovering attentively somewhere above the biographical story. The biographical narrator who hovers thus invisibly, mysteriously implying speech even in his silence, is an illusion created not by the *Life* but by an inadequate model of narrative structure.

The example of Boswell in his role as biographical narrator is in fact a particularly suggestive one, for it allows us to see that an antithetical model of structure does not compel us to ignore anything that we should want to explain in more conventional terms. When we say that Boswell in that role is something like a major character in a drama, for instance, or that the world of his consciousness is only one of the separate worlds contained within the *Life*, we simply account in more precise terms for what we otherwise want to call his mediating perspective: now it is not that the world of the story merely exists independent of his consciousness, but that he is continuously responding to it, measuring himself against it, in just the same way as the inhabitants of that world react to each other.

This is a notion not altogether foreign. We appeal to it, for example, when we attempt to explain the growing involvement of the narrator in *Troilus and Criseyde* in the story he is telling, his dwindling detachment and anxious interventions, and we perhaps do the same to a lesser degree whenever we discuss aesthetic distance in narrative.[5] Yet the structure of the *Life* itself demands that we confront the problem of Boswell's role as narrator in terms more direct than this, for viewed in the light of our usual model of narrative structure Boswell is the most obtrusive of narrators, constantly giving his own opinions, correcting the assertions of characters within the story, commenting, qualifying, dwelling on his own concerns—in short, making his own presence as visible as that of the story he is telling.

When we mistakenly view Boswell as a mediating presence hovering somewhere above the world of the story, we have no choice but to see all this as inexplicable intrusion,

---

[5] See Paul K. Alkon, "Boswell's Control of Aesthetic Distance," *University of Toronto Quarterly* (January 1969), 174-91.

a usurpation of narrative space belonging by right to Johnson and the world he inhabits (it is an inadequate model
of narrative structure that creates the illusion of "right"
here, however).[6] When we see Boswell as a narrator so to
speak on the same level as his story, on the other hand, we
simultaneously see the explanation we seek: it is Boswell's
obsessive fascination with the world he is describing, his
anxious and continuous need to measure himself against
its norms, that explains his visibility as a narrator; the
otherness, the self-contained separateness of that world is a
condition of his visibility.

Yet in responding this way to the world dominated by
Johnson's moral and intellectual presence, in being so
often moved to anxious self-assertion and self-justification,
Boswell is doing nothing essentially different from almost
every other inhabitant of the *Life*: the Johnson who awes
learned men into silence through fear of competing with
him in conversation, who speaks and writes with magisterial
and penetrating authority on all matters of the human
mind and heart, who even in the torments of his religious
uncertainty is a figure larger than life, this Johnson is a
creature equally compelling and intimidating, a threat to
all lesser worlds of opinion and belief. It is simply because
Boswell's narration occupies so much space in the *Life*,
giving us a full view of one anxious response to that threat,
that it calls such attention to itself.

To see the world of Boswell's narrative consciousness as
a separate world in the *Life* is once again to begin by seeing
that the structure of the narrative fractures along the divi-
sions of what we normally call mediation. To explain the
coherence of Boswell's consciousness as a self-contained
world, the sense in which it embodies its own norms and

[6] An extreme form of this error would be to take the *Life* as auto-
biography operating on false pretenses. This view, once associated
with Percy Fitzgerald, has recently been resuscitated and given modern
dress by Richard B. Schwartz in *Boswell's Johnson: A Preface to the
Life* (Madison: University of Wisconsin Press, 1978).

obeys its own laws of perception, we once again need to invoke the notion of an abstract continuum of structural possibilities. Now, however, we shall want to complete that reversal of perspective that I initiated by taking the purely antithetical structure of drama as a primary model for explaining the structure of the *Life*. The world of Boswell's narrative consciousness moves us, in its inner coherence and separateness, to what has become the remote extreme of the continuum, to the model of literary structure represented in lyric poetry.

There has always been a sense in which lyric structure, giving us a world wholly absorbed into the speaker's consciousness, has operated as a model to set off narrator from narrative, the storyteller from the story he is telling. In taking the character of Miss Bridget as a pretext for a more general commentary on human delusions and self-delusions, the narrator of *Tom Jones* is after all only imitating the movement of the speaker in "To His Coy Mistress" from the naked reality of an attempted seduction to a meditation on time, death, and eternity. Narrative structure is defined by what is left behind: Miss Bridget and her world go on existing, and to it the narrator will in time return. This is a movement that is again and again imitated in the *Life*, creating the illusion that we are dealing with conventional narrative, or, more precisely, with narrative that may be explained in entirely conventional terms.

When we explain the structure of the *Life* in antithetical terms, however, the invocation of lyric as a model moves us toward an opposing perspective: Boswell as narrator, enclosed within a world of consciousness or perception floating free of everything else in the story, resembles the speaker of a lyric poem precisely in his epistemological imprisonment, his isolation from all worlds other than his own. And what completes this isolation is that there is in the *Life* nothing corresponding to that stable reality that in *Tom Jones* we call the world of the story, only a galaxy of separate worlds existing in relation to each other as world and antiworld.

Something like a final implication of our taking seriously Derrida's notion of the structurality of structure, or of explaining the structure of the *Life* as a system of negative differences with no positive or substantial worlds, is that in the end we discover no model adequate to the demands of explanation. The epistemological model we invoke when we attempt to deal with the problem of mediating perspective, the abstract structural possibilities we call upon when we attempt to locate the *Life* on an ideal continuum of literary forms, even the Saussurean model we introduce in describing the *Life* as a structure of antitheses, all these are partial and unsatisfactory lenses through which we gaze at a phenomenal reality existing on its own infinitely complex terms.

This is something of what Barthes has in mind when he speaks of abandoning the search for a model transcendent to the text, of treating the text as its own model. Yet even this perspective, which at least allows us to glimpse in the *Life* the collision of world and antiworld, the assertion and subversion of norms, is not finally adequate to our purposes. For it is not really as though the *Life* has assimilated models or elements of models external to itself only to subject them, under the pressure of its antithetical energies, to subversion or dissolution. It is that the notion of the text as its own model reveals to us as in a mirror the inadequacies of our attempts at explanation.

An attempt to explain the structure of the *Life* must ultimately bring under scrutiny the very notion of what it means to use a model in literary interpretation. When we have no clear idea of what is involved, our tendency is perhaps to think of a series or sequence of models that brings us ever closer to a true description of the state of affairs we are attempting to explain, much as a series of unsatisfactory models of DNA structure led biology (in the persons of

Watson and Crick) to a model corresponding to the actual structure of DNA. The notion is an attractive one; it seems to explain, for instance, why we can go a certain distance by comparing the *Life* with the *Odyssey* or *Tom Jones*, or comparing its structure to that of drama or lyric—but it contains in the end a fatal weakness.

The weakness is this: whenever we invoke a model approximating the structure of the *Life*, we are explaining not that structure but the model itself (if we had a model exactly corresponding to the structure of the *Life*, models would become unnecessary, for then we should have succeeded in duplicating the structure we set out to explain). If Derrida's vision of the structurality of structure suggests an antithetical model for the *Life*, we understand its status only when we call attention to the modelness of the model: it too is merely a model, and bears the same relation to the text as any other (and this is so even when it allows us to explain the *Life* in clearer terms than other models).

In a very real sense, deconstructivist interpretation as it is being developed now by such writers as Geoffrey Hartman and Hillis Miller is explanation not of literature and language but of the deconstructivist model of literature and language—or, at least, of a system of assumptions that could be represented by a model. It is the strangeness of the model, and the sense of dizzying infinitude that it induces, that leads to the notion of interpretation as an autonomous activity, as a free and infinite play of signification. Though he does not put it in just these terms—interpretation as the explanation of a model—this is what M. H. Abrams is trying to deal with in some recent remarks on deconstructivist interpretation:

> What is one to say in response to this abysmal vision of the textual world of literature, philosophy, and all the other achievements of mankind in the medium of language? There is, I think, only one adequate response, and that is the one that William Blake made to the Angel in

The Marriage of Heaven and Hell. After they had groped their way down a "winding cavern," the Angel revealed to Blake a ghastly vision of hell as an "infinite Abyss"; in it was "the sun, black but shining," around which were "fiery tracks on which revolved vast spiders." But no sooner, says Blake, had "my friend the Angel" departed, "then this appearance was no more, but I found myself sitting on a pleasant bank beside a river by moon light, hearing a harper who sung to a harp." The Angel, "surprised asked me how I escaped? I answered: 'All that we saw was owing to your metaphysics.' "[7]

To view the structure of the *Life* as a system of antithetical relations is to raise just the sort of specter Abrams describes: our usual model of narrative structure at least allowed us the comfort of perceiving the *Life* as a world entire in itself, as a sphere of phenomenal reality substantial in its own terms, and this is just what an antithetical model of structure seems to dissolve. And yet the world of the *Life* continues to seem substantial in the old way: "Upon the much-expected Wednesday, I called on him about half an hour before dinner, as I often did when we were to dine out together, to see that he was ready in time, and to accompany him. I found him buffeting his books, as upon a former occasion, covered with dust, and making no preparation for going abroad. 'How is this, Sir? (said I.) Don't you recollect that you are to dine at Mr. Dilly's?' " (III.66-67).

When Boswell breaks into speech, becoming a character in the scene he was describing an instant ago, do we not after all have that chasm between worlds that the notion of antithetical structure is meant to explain? For it is true that the world of speech will within a few moments expand into a reality independent of Boswell's consciousness, giving us an unmediated reality—the reality of Johnson and

7 M. H. Abrams, "The Deconstructive Angel," *Critical Inquiry*, 3 (Spring 1977) 436-37.

Wilkes talking directly to each other, with another Boswell present only as an inhabitant of their world—that we want to explain in terms of its otherness, its antithetical relation to the world contained in Boswell's perception of things. Yet may we explain any of this without dissolving both worlds into unreality, into that system of negative relations demanded by our model?

The answer is that we may, but only when we begin by seeing that our model is only a model, not an object of explanation but a means to explanation. For the model tells us that the positive existence or substantiality of the world contained in Boswell's consciousness ("I found him buffeting his books, as upon a former occasion, covered with dust") is a momentary illusion created by that invisible system of negative relations that defines its existence. It is real only by virtue of what it is not. It is not, for example, the world revealed in the *Prayers and Meditations* or in the conversation scenes, and when we have gone full circle through the system of negative relations there is nothing remaining to be called a world. Yet in going full circle through that system we shall be explaining not the structure of the *Life* but the model we invoke to explain it.

It is the structure of the *Life* itself that remains when we have exhausted the resources of our model, and when we see this we see what it is about that structure that gave the model its power of explanation. It is precisely because every world within the *Life* can be seen as substantial in its turn, that each retains the potentiality of positive existence even as we describe it in terms of a system of negative relations, that we want to continue to view the *Life* as a whole, as a coherent sphere of phenomenal reality—as, in short, a literary world. What the model shows us, before it has done its duty and must be discarded as giving us only an approximate account of what we want to explain, is that within the *Life* the laws of coherence are laws of antithetical relation.

To explain the *Life* in terms of world and antiworld, to throw light into one or another area in that vast system of antithetical relations that is its narrative and thematic structure, is to return in the end to a version of the same conception of literary structure that has always been posited in objective interpretation. At the moment when we gaze at the structure of the *Life* as it actually exists, our explanatory models collapse in upon themselves and disappear, and what we have now is a clear vision of what we saw before only obscurely: the total world of wit and intellectual passion and high comedy, of spiritual isolation and solitary suffering, that is dominated by the gigantic presence of Samuel Johnson.

THREE

STRUCTURE AND ABSENCE

THE problems posed by the structure of the *Life of Johnson* seem to revolve around another problem that we do not at first glance see in structural terms: the tension between various idealized versions of Johnson that dominate the foreground of the biographical story and the darker and more disturbing Johnson we glimpse in its gloomy background. The problem is a problem because neither Johnson is wholly unreal: the image of the revered sage and moralist is not an arbitrary fiction imposed by Johnson's admirers on some gloomy and contrary reality. There is much in Johnson's writings and conversation, in his literary and moral character, to sustain the image, and yet that gloomy and contrary reality exists as well, inhabited by a Johnson quite unlike the image the world has created of him.

Even to speak of the foreground of the biographical story, however, or of a gloomy background occasionally glimpsed, is to impose upon the *Life* itself an illusion of perspective. The implication is that in passing through the foreground—the conversation scenes, say, with their image of Johnson in exuberant good spirits—to the darker realm of existence that lies behind them, we have penetrated through appearances to reality, or at least to a reality more real than what we have passed through. Thus the notion of pictorial perspective translates into moral and existential terms; in the depths of the biographical story we glimpse the Johnson who suffers throughout his life from a dismal malady of the spirit, from that "dejection, gloom, and despair, which made existence misery" (I.63).

There is much in the narrative structure of the *Life* to sustain this illusion, but the reason we do not immediately seek to explain it in structural terms is that it is ultimately sustained by something else. In every biographical narrative perhaps, but in the *Life* overwhelmingly, the illusion of receding perspective derives from an idea of actual or ideal presence: somewhere behind the *Life*, glimpsed only imperfectly in any moment of narration or speech, seen in terms sometimes more real or less superficial than others, lies the presence of a Samuel Johnson not identical with or reducible to the text we are reading. As we seem to pierce through language to the world it describes, we seem to penetrate, or always to be on the point of penetrating, through the *Life* to a Johnsonian presence.

Yet it is not altogether an illusion of visual perspective that imposes this on us, for that perspective is itself an illusion: we gaze into the painted landscape aware that there is, there behind the tiny receding figure trudging into the distance down a disappearing road, nothing but canvas. The illusion perhaps corresponds to a reality in which background becomes foreground, where as we ourselves move down a road the scene changes and a new landscape looms before us, but even this has something in common with what we have been calling illusion; the new landscape too has its foreground and its background, and this, in just the same way as in the landscape on the wall, reaches out to infinity.

The meaning of the analogous illusion in the *Life*, an illusion of ontological rather than visual perspective, lies in that which the illusion exists to shut out or deny. For unless we could in some sense pierce through the *Life* to the actual or ideal presence of Johnson, to a reality at least implied by the illusion of receding perspective, the *Life* would seem to be nothing more than a window on infinity, a biographical portrait of no subject. As the word corresponds to the object it names, biography must correspond to a biographical subject external to its narrative, the *Life* to a Johnson not contained within the pages of the *Life*.

The notion of a Johnsonian presence behind the text of

the *Life* may serve to explain an odd confusion in Boswell's mind about the nature of the story he is telling. In a purely conventional sense, Boswell understands Johnson's death as a kind of absence; those who have contributed to his account of Johnson's life, he says in the opening pages, resemble *"the grateful tribes of ancient nations, of which every individual was eager to throw a stone upon the grave of a departed Hero, and thus to share in the pious office of erecting an honourable monument to his memory"* (I.5). Yet this is only absence from the world of men, and biography is another sort of world.

It is always the world of his biography that Boswell has in mind when he writes as though Johnson, though absent through death in some trivial or literal sense, lives on in the *Life*—as though, that is, the soul had departed the corpse only to take up lodging in the Johnsonian presence behind the story: "Had his other friends been as diligent and ardent as I was, he might have been almost entirely preserved. As it is, I will venture to say that he will be seen in this work more completely than any man who has ever yet lived" (I.30). For what is preserved, if we grant the existence of the corpse, is the soul or spirit that once resided in it.

Yet there seems to be something mistaken, too, about dismissing all this as mere illusion, asserting that there is nothing behind the *Life* but the absence of any biographical subject not contained in the text. For while there is nothing we could point to behind the text, as we might utter a word and point to the object it named, there is a stubborn complexity in the illusion of Johnson's presence that invites us to consider it in more detail. What teases us about the notion of absence, of a vacuum at the center of the *Life*, is that it is made meaningful by an earlier notion of presence; it is not absence pure and simple—if that is in any case conceivable—but absence of what the *Life* projects as a presence.

The notion of an ideal or abstract center, that is to say,

is something equally posited by the opposing notions of presence and absence; in a manner of speaking they converge on it. For to say that there is a vacuum at the center of the *Life* is to say that that center exists after all. The emptiness of the conjurer's hat when he has completed the trick is defined by the trick itself: hats are normally empty, and emptiness so to speak signifies only when we expect to see a rabbit. The problem of absence in the *Life* is thus simultaneously a problem of presence, and it is this that leads one to explore the problem in terms of narrative and thematic structure.

When we approach the problem through a consideration of structure, we discover that we are regarding from a new angle the puzzle of receding perspective in the narrative, the illusion of a gloomy background occasionally glimpsed behind the conviviality and bustle of the foreground. For what that receding perspective implies is nothing other than the center we wish to locate: if idealized versions of Johnson dominate the foreground of the *Life*, and if behind these we glimpse a bleaker reality inhabited by another Johnson, our very notion of reality, of what is selective and idealized as opposed to complete and substantial, involves the notion of a Johnsonian presence somewhere behind that last reality, a center on which everything in the story somehow converges.

To say that idealized versions of Johnson dominate the foreground of the *Life* is, at the same time, to say that we recognize these as being creations, unreal figments for one or another reason constructed by the inhabitants of Johnson's world. In general terms, we want to say that we recognize these as selective or idealized constructions because they conflict or are at odds with other elements of the story, but this does not account for our sense that they obscure a more substantial reality. It is not a matter of competing versions of an identical reality, as one might hear, say, in courtroom testimony, but of realities competing with one another.

69

The illusion of receding moral and ontological perspective in the *Life* is created by this competition, or rather by
the terms on which it is played out within the structure of
the narrative. For every idealized version of Johnson originates in some distinct world of consciousness or perception, and to recognize it as an idealized creation or construction is nothing other than to see that the world to
which it belongs is threatened or subverted by antiworlds
containing radically different conceptions of Johnson. To
isolate the relation of world and antiworld in the *Life*, or
to say that its structure exists as a network of antithetical
relations, is to represent that structure in frozen or spatial
terms; the dynamic element that completes the account
lies in the concept of deconstruction.

Our sense of structure and meaning in the *Life*, that is, is
not anything frozen or spatial; it is something that emerges
only as the narrative assumes its shape as a whole. And it
is the dynamics of this process—the narrative logic governing our sense of structure and meaning—that demands to
be seen in terms of deconstruction, with one world of consciousness or perception dissolving or giving way to another
in the antithetical regions behind it, moving us inward to
an implied center in which, or just behind which, we shall
discover the Johnsonian presence corresponding to perceptions of Johnson. It is not that one deconstructs the idealized versions of Johnson that dominate the foreground of
the story, but that explanation mirrors the process through
which they are deconstructed within the text itself.

At this point, perhaps, I should abandon the metaphor
of receding or pictorial perspective in the *Life*; it is simply
a metaphor, and has only the limited virtue of allowing
one to speak about something actually occurring within
the structure of the *Life*. Yet explanation must nonetheless
begin in what the metaphor led me to call the foreground
of the biographical story, with one or another of those
idealized perceptions of Johnson that seem to dissolve in
the dark light of antithetical relation. This is the signifi-

cance, for instance, of the long passage from Courtenay's poem on Johnson's moral and literary character that Boswell quotes early in the narrative:

> 'By nature's gifts ordain'd mankind to rule,
> He, like a Titian, form'd his brilliant school;
> And taught congenial spirits to excel,
> While from his lips impressive wisdom fell.

. . . .

> Nor was his energy confin'd alone
> To friends around his philosophick throne;
> *Its influence wide improv'd our letter'd isle,*
> *And lucid vigour mark'd the general style:*
> As Nile's proud waves, swoln from their oozy bed,
> First o'er the neighbouring meads majestick spread;
> Till gathering force, they more and more expand,
> And with new virtue fertilise the land.'
>
> (I.222-23)

The occasion for bringing Courtenay's idealized vision of Johnson into the *Life* at this point is ostensibly Boswell's consideration of Johnson's style: the italicized couplet simply repeats in rhyme and pentameter Boswell's own pedestrian comments on Johnson's prose—"from the influence which he has had upon our composition, scarcely any thing is written now that is not better expressed than was usual before he appeared to lead the national taste." Yet italicization at this moment comes close to reversing its normal significance: if it is *only* that couplet in Courtenay's poem that supports Boswell's point, what is the burden of meaning carried by the unitalicized lines, the image of Johnson that now floats disembodied above Boswell's discussion of prose style?

The answer is that Johnson's prose style is transparently a pretext for establishing, thus early in the story, an image of Johnson that dominates the entire foreground of the *Life*. The true subject of Courtenay's poem is an invisible

71

monarchy of mind and moral vision, a world in which Johnson sits high above ordinary mankind dispensing wisdom, in both speech and writing, from a philosophic throne. And this image, long after it has dissolved in favor of darker and more complex perceptions of Johnson, continues to exert something of its original power. It is why, for instance, we will see Johnson's famous meeting with George III as a meeting between two monarchs—even, when Johnson is speaking, as a meeting between a monarch in the realm of mind and one of his ordinary subjects.

In the metaphor of a circle of congenial spirits surrounding Johnson's philosophic throne we discover too an image that seems to expand and stabilize Courtenay's idealized portrait. For this is a metaphor that the *Life* seems to enact: throughout the story, as kindred spirits like Reynolds, Beauclerk, Langton, and numberless others are drawn toward Johnson's presence as by a moral or intellectual law of gravity, we do see something like a monarchy of intellect emerge. The inhabitants of the *Life*, no matter how talented or considerable in their own right, do revolve around Johnson like greater or lesser bodies around a sun, and from this the image of a philosophic throne, a fixed or stationary point from which the world comes and goes, takes on its significance.

Within the invisible circumference of Johnson's world in the *Life* exist all those who perceive him as an object of awe and veneration. And even when we see that every such conception of Johnson originates in a distinct world of consciousness, the consciousness of a Reynolds, a Langton, a Beauclerk, a Campbell, we still want to say that the foreground of the *Life* is dominated by a galaxy of worlds related to one another by something like the idealizing impulse expressed in pure form in Courtenay's lines. The monarchy of mind and moral vision in this sense exists almost as the poem describes it, and the *Life* is populated by its subjects.

Yet even to say that Courtenay's image of Johnson is

idealized is to perceive that it inevitably dissolves in the light of antithetical relation, that his poem exists as a world in relation to antiworlds working towards its deconstruction. Here, once again, the blankness of the page separating Boswell's commentary from Courtenay's verse signals an antithetical system of relations, for Boswell's more complex consciousness of Johnson includes darker elements that Courtenay's image simply denies or excludes, and the same is true of Reynolds, Langton, and the rest of those congenial spirits whom Courtenay portrays as the subjects of Johnson's invisible monarchy. The whiteness of the page that surrounds Courtenay's poem signals its isolation within an entire network of darker and more complex conceptions of Johnson, and in its isolation it wavers and begins to fade.

The reason we want to say that the foreground of the *Life* is dominated by a galaxy of worlds that seem to expand and stabilize Courtenay's image, then, is merely because that image corresponds to the unreal figments existing in the minds of those who first know Johnson only through his writings—to Boswell's imaginary sage, living in a state of solemn elevated abstraction in the immense metropolis of London, to Langton's remarkably decorous philosopher, to the magisterial presence Reynolds imagines to exist behind the pages of the *Life of Savage*. Yet these are figments that dissolve in light of the uncouth and troubling reality of Johnson's actual presence, and in the moment of their dissolution there occurs a simultaneous dissolution of Courtenay's image of an invisible monarchy.

Yet throughout the *Life* a shadow of that monarchy remains. To see that Boswell's or Reynolds's consciousness of Johnson contains disturbing elements denied by Courtenay's image—a Johnson who mutters to himself in company, who gesticulates constantly and ludicrously, who eats with such unwholesome voracity that the veins in his forehead swell—is indeed to begin a pursuit of the series of deconstructions that carries us inward toward the center of the

73

Life, toward that bleak and gloomy realm of private suffering revealed in the *Prayers and Meditations.* Yet, through all this, the idealizing impulse shared by Courtenay and such congenial spirits as Boswell and Reynolds persists.

To understand why the impulse persists, we must glance in a preliminary way at a principle that organizes the structure of the *Life* as a whole, and that the deconstructive sequence leading to its center brings into ever greater visibility. In brief, the congenial spirits who surround Johnson's philosophic throne in the *Life* are creatures of an age of spiritual disintegration whose own longing for moral certitude impels them to construct a Johnson who does not exist, to hear in Johnson's speech and his writings a tone of magisterial reassurance to which, in their anxiety, they supply a corresponding presence. The imaginary throne of Courtenay's poem is, so to speak, empty throughout the *Life,* and only within the separate consciousness of every congenial spirit does it come to be occupied by an unreal and idealized Johnson.

The *Life* as a whole enacts a drama of presence and absence at least partly because the same drama is played out within the consciousness of those of its inhabitants who perceive Johnson as an object of awe and veneration. To imagine the Johnson who speaks in *Rasselas* or *The Rambler* as an idealized philosopher or sage is to imagine a presence behind the moral voice, and to greet the uncouth figure in unbuckled shoes and shriveled wig is to understand suddenly that that presence is imaginary after all, that there is quite literally nothing there where one had imagined an elevated and serene moralist. And yet the idealizing impulse is not defeated but only thwarted; contrary realities are adjusted to one another, and perceptions of Johnson antithetical in their nature compete within the problematic space of the real.

There is a danger here of seeming to generalize the experience of only a few major characters in the *Life*—Boswell's, certainly, and Reynolds's and Langton's, and perhaps

Oglethorpe's or Campbell's or Burney's, but who then? Yet the pattern of their experience is universal for those whom the *Life* counts as subjects of its invisible monarchy: in one way or another, kindred spirits are drawn toward Johnson's actual presence as by a law of moral or intellectual gravity, a process that invariably begins in a reverence for the disembodied voice heard in the writings and ends in the reality of quite another Johnson holding forth in drawing room or tavern. And if this other Johnson gives grounds at all for awe or veneration, it is only as he distantly resembles the wholly imaginary moralist and sage.

What is also universal in the *Life*, dividing its world into an inner and on outer sphere, is the shared sense of spiritual crisis that impels those who venerate Johnson to seek in his presence a refuge from a world of abstract conflict, of growing anxiety and doubt. To perceive Johnson as an heroic spirit fighting a solitary battle against the forces of skepticism and infidelity—the forces of Voltaire and Hume and Holbach and a thousand minor philosophes and freethinkers—and to discover in his writings and his speech a power of gigantic moral reassurance in the midst of overwhelming doubt, is simultaneously to perceive the age in the same light as so many nineteenth-century writers would come to perceive their own, as a time in which "old opinions, feelings—ancestral customs and institutions are crumbling away, and both the spiritual and the temporal worlds are darkened by the shadow of change."[1]

It is this perception of the age, as we shall see when we come to discuss the problem of audience in the *Life*, that sustains the image of an invisible monarchy, and that locates those who perceive Johnson as a moral hero within the inner sphere of its world. For whatever they do not have in common, inhabitants of the outer sphere do share not merely a failure to see Johnson as an object of veneration,

[1] Edward Bulwer Lytton, *England and the English,* quoted in Walter E. Houghton, *The Victorian Frame of Mind* (New Haven: Yale University Press, 1957) p. 2.

but a benign or optimistic view of the age. From the cheerful stoicism of Hume to the vacant cheerfulness of Johnson's schoolfellow Mr. Hector, from the idiosyncratic preoccupation of Lord Monboddo to the pagan insouciance of John Wilkes, those who see Johnson as merely an odd or opinionated creature do so because they are simply oblivious to the moral context in which he figures as a hero.

Since the invisible law of gravity drawing kindred spirits toward Johnson's actual presence begins to operate only at the moment one imagines an idealized and disembodied Johnson as a presence behind his writings, we should expect that those writings, at least, would serve within the structure of the *Life* to sustain the idealized image. For though the uncouth figure who greets Boswell or Langton at the door of his chambers shatters the illusion they had carried in their minds to the encounter, the illusion should at least return with full force when one goes back to the pages out of which it was created. And, on one level, this is precisely what occurs; whenever he rereads *Rasselas*, says Boswell, gazing back over his long acquaintance with Johnson to the first time he read Johnson's works, "I can scarcely believe that I had the honour of enjoying the intimacy of such a man" (I.342).

The Johnson whose intimacy Boswell enjoyed is not, of course, the Johnson whom he rediscovers whenever he opens the pages of *Rasselas*, for at the moment he begins to read his acquaintance with an actual Johnson, the Johnson of drawing room and tavern, is annihilated. The Johnson whose voice he hears in *Rasselas* is precisely that disembodied sage and moralist who awakens his veneration— grown up in his imagination, as he says, into a kind of superstitious reverence—when he is a young man in Edinburgh. It is a short circuit of the imagination that returns the middle-aged Boswell, a survivor gazing retrospectively on Johnson and the world he has departed, to that state of superstitious reverence in which he came down from Edinburgh to London as a youth of twenty-two.

In the pattern of Boswell's experience, then, we should expect to discover a pattern that serves to explain the structure of the *Life* as a whole. For it is not simply the case that Boswell's experience is the experience of everyone who inhabits the inner sphere of the *Life*, that so many others have been drawn by the disembodied and idealized Johnson of the writings into the presence of an actual Johnson, but rather that the disembodied sage and moralist lives on when the actual Johnson is in the grave. Whenever Johnson's works enter the *Life*, the assumed audience of the biographical story in one sense reenacts just the same experience: like Boswell or Reynolds or Langton before them, its members move from the disembodied moralist into the presence of a Johnson who moves and speaks in actual surroundings, and the idealized presence they imagine to exist behind the writings lingers in the memory, coloring what actually occurs in the drawing room.

To say that Johnson's writings compose a separate world within the *Life* is to see them as allowing an unmediated view of the imaginary philosopher whose magisterial voice provides moral reassurance in an age of spiritual anxiety. Yet the passages from Johnson's writings that Boswell quotes throughout the *Life* do not themselves compose a world. The reason we want to speak of them that way is precisely that we glimpse, as the invisible context of any passage quoted in the *Life*, the unquoted totality of Johnson's writings, a separate and coherent sphere of mind and moral imagination. The passages interpolated in the text are an assemblage of reminders, and we reach through their final configuration to a world.

Always in the *Life*, I have said, the mechanics of quotation—quotation marks, textual spacings, margins, differences of type—represent the text calling attention to its own discontinuities. Typography, in itself neutral and meaningless, points to the underlying reality of an antithetical system. For it is the system or structure of antithetical relations that gives the typographical form of the

77

text its meaning, that in a manner of speaking allows the quotation mark or the blankness of the page to signify. And though they signify equally whenever the *Life* interpolates a letter or a secondhand account of Johnson or a passage from the *Prayers and Meditations,* they signify whenever we encounter a passage from *The Rambler* or *Rasselas* or *The Vanity of Human Wishes* the presence of a world not only separate from but alien to the text.

The very meaning of quotation in a narrative like the *Life,* and of the mechanics that set off or signal the otherness of what is quoted, derives from what Hillis Miller has called "the inexorable law which makes the uncanny, 'undecidable,' or 'alogical' relation of host and parasite, heterogeneity within homogeneity . . . reform itself within each separate entity which had seemed, on the larger scale, to be one or the other."[2] Even when we view the *Life* as a single coherent world, we understand that passages from Johnson's writings belong to and have been detached from another world and brought into the text: it is an element of another world that the blank space surrounding the passage proclaims, and that is what is signaled by the marks of quotation in the text.

When we have seen that the world of the *Life* is not single and coherent, that it dissolves into a system of separate worlds existing in antithetical relation to one another, any direct quotation of Johnson's writings within the text raises a more complex problem. To say that a series of lines from *The Vanity of Human Wishes* exists in antithetical relation to Boswell's perception of Johnson, for instance, and that this relation is precisely what is signaled by the blankness of the page separating Boswell's commentary on the poem from Johnson's magnificent lines, is implicitly to assert that *The Vanity of Human Wishes* works to dissolve or deconstruct Boswell's idealizing perception of Johnson. Yet this Johnson, the stern and clairvoyant moralist

[2] Miller, "The Critic as Host," p. 434.

speaking eloquently of the inevitable misery of human existence, is identical with the disembodied philosopher who awakened Boswell's impulse to veneration long before he made the acquaintance of any other Johnson.

What is true of Boswell in his relation to Johnson's writings, moreover, is true for every other member of the inner circle of the *Life*: the idealized Johnson who dwells in the separate consciousness of a Reynolds or a Langton or a Burke is the moralist of *Rasselas* and *The Vanity of Human Wishes*, the imaginary Johnson whose mind and moral character moved them to seek out the actual Johnson of drawing room and tavern. This is the meaning, for instance, of the passage Boswell quotes not from *Rasselas* or *The Vanity of Human Wishes* but from Johnson's preface to his early translation of Lobo's *Voyage to Abyssinia*:

'The reader will here find no regions cursed with irremediable barrenness, or blessed with spontaneous fecundity. . . . Here are no Hottentots without religious polity or articulate language; no Chinese perfectly polite, and completely skilled in all sciences; he will discover, what will always be discovered by a diligent and impartial enquirer, that wherever human nature is to be found, there is a mixture of vice and virtue, a contest of passion and reason; and that the Creator doth not appear partial in his distributions, but has balanced, in most countries, their particular inconveniencies by particular favours.' (I.89)

The biographical reason for bringing the passage into the *Life* is obvious enough: here, in a preface written when Johnson is young and impoverished and unknown, working in thankless obscurity as a provincial bookseller's hack, is the same voice that will be heard later in the poetry and the moral writings and the great philosophical passages of the *Lives of the Poets*. Yet the thematic significance of the passage is quite removed from its place in the biographical

79

story, for what it celebrates is the sudden emergence of that idealized moralist who will come to dwell in the consciousness of those who surround the actual Johnson in his world. "Mr. Edmund Burke," says Boswell by way of introducing the passage, ". . . was, I remember, much delighted with the following specimen." Burke's delight, like Boswell's, is the delight of a world that has discovered a monarch to set upon a philosophic throne hitherto vacant.

Yet it is not so far obvious why the voice of Johnson the moralist is heard by men like Boswell and Burke as a voice of moral reassurance. There is, to be sure, an evident faith in an ontological order both rational and providential ("the Creator doth not appear partial in his distributions"), but nothing to suggest that this goes beyond a piety wholly conventional. The answer seems to lie, rather, in the power of the moralist to penetrate the shifting appearances of human life, to brush aside delusion and self-delusion and bring into view the permanent and universal reality beneath the surface. What we see, what is seen by Boswell and Burke, is what is always there to be seen by "a diligent and impartial enquirer, that wherever human nature is to be found, there is a mixture of vice and virtue."

Yet this too is an observation wholly conventional in eighteenth-century terms, the central assumption of Pope's *Essay on Man* and *Gulliver's Travels*, of *Tom Jones* and *Tristram Shandy*, of the ethical doctrines of Shaftesbury and the comedies of Goldsmith and Sheridan. What, then, allows Boswell and Burke to hear the voice of the moralist in so unlikely a context as this, a preface to a translation of Lobo in which Johnson is, on the face of it, merely attacking the literary tradition of the fabulous voyage? The answer is that all this has only superficially to do with fabulous books of travel, brutish Hottentots and polite Chinese, for the standard against which they are measured is the universal reality of human nature in all ages and countries —what will *always* be discovered—as seen through study and observation, what a traveler must know before he sets out on his travels.

Whenever Johnson's writings appear in the *Life*, each passage floating in a textual space that compels us to see it as a specimen momentarily detached from the larger body of his thought, we again encounter, whatever the subject, a penetrating moral vision that sweeps aside illusory appearances and insists on a permanent and universal truth. Johnson the moralist is an Augustan survivor, the last great spokesman for a moral and literary tradition reaching back through Renaissance humanism to classical antiquity. Behind every specimen quoted in the *Life* there lies, there in the unquoted totality of Johnson's writings, the entire authority of the Augustan vision:

> A great part of the time of those who are placed at the greatest distance by fortune, or by temper, must unavoidably pass in the same manner; and though, when the claims of nature are satisfied, caprice, and vanity, and accident, begin to produce discriminations and peculiarities, yet the eye is not very heedful or quick, which cannot discover the same causes still terminating their influence in the same effects, though sometimes accelerated, sometimes retarded, or perplexed by multiplied combinations. We are all prompted by the same motives, all deceived by the same fallacies, all animated by hope, obstructed by danger, entangled by desire, and seduced by pleasure. (*Rambler* 60)

The power of reassurance in Johnson's writings, then, and the power of the imaginary and idealized moralist to awaken the veneration of lesser souls, derives in the last analysis from the ontological assumptions underlying the view of human nature embodied in those writings. For in continually reminding humanity that there are no individual hopes and fears, that the disguises of life—social rank, wealth, power, age, country—are separable and adventitious, that the interior existence of man is common to every soul on earth and in history, the disembodied moralist invokes a larger principle of intelligibility, an explanation of the universe for which classical and Christian myth, philosophical and theological systems, are merely grand metaphors.

Unlike the Johnson of drawing room and tavern, moving through the dirty streets of London in an age growing increasingly troubled, Johnson the sage and moralist is a dweller in the city of God, an observer of human existence who seems, amid the anxiety and skepticism and doubt of lesser souls, sustained by the same large sense of spiritual unity that sustained Augustine or Aquinas. And if the moralist draws an uncompromisingly gloomy picture of human life, portrays it as a realm of delusion and misery, his explanation is implicitly the same as theirs: the misery of our existence is a misery of alienation from the divine, that derangement of the will and enslavement to the passions that Christian theology expresses in the doctrine of original sin.

When we perceive Johnson's writings as a separate world within the *Life*, they do suggest in overpowering terms a sense of spiritual coherence and even, at the deepest level, of moral serenity. The disembodied and magisterial Johnson they project is real, and only when we hear the tones of moral serenity in his voice do we fully understand why he so assuages the doubt and anxiety of lesser souls. Thus, for instance, when Boswell comes to discuss *The Vanity of Human Wishes*, he omits altogether to quote the long first part of the poem, that great and gloomy picture of human existence as an unrelieved round of misery and delusion. The page is occupied instead by the conclusion, a picture of the universe as governed by divine love and wisdom: " 'These goods he grants, who grants the power to gain; / With these celestial wisdom calms the mind, / And makes the happiness she does not find' " (I.195).

With celestial wisdom, too, Johnson the moralist calms

the mind; "were all the other excellencies of this poem annihilated," says Boswell, "it must ever have our grateful
reverence from its noble conclusion." Yet the *Life* as a
whole always insists that we read *The Vanity of Human
Wishes* from a reverse perspective, see its gloomy picture of
human misery as overwhelming and finally negating the
conventional pieties of the conclusion Boswell sees as being
so noble. The poem that haunts the *Life* is a *Vanity of
Human Wishes* in which the conclusion is what is annihilated, the bleak vision of the suppressed earlier lines moving in to occupy a textual space suddenly vacant. The poem
that haunts the *Life* is a poem that simply ends with the
lines occurring at the beginning of the specimen Boswell
quotes: " 'Must helpless man, in ignorance sedate, / Roll
darkling down the torrent of his fate?' "

The terrible question posed in those lines must be answered either in the negative or the affirmative, and the
answer that pervades the *Life* is the affirmative: we must, in
ignorance sedate, roll darkling down the torrent of our
fate. It is Johnson's gigantic power of affirmation as a
moralist that allows Boswell to dwell serenely on the poem's
concluding lines, that allows others in Johnson's world to
discover in his writings a voice that annihilates skepticism
and doubt, creating at least for the moment a comforting
illusion of moral certitude. Yet to do this is to exclude an
alternative possibility inexorably suggested by the writings
themselves, the possibility that they are written out of a
personal sense of misery and despair that wholly overwhelms conventional piety and outworn mythologies of
divine and universal order.

In this instance, *The Vanity of Human Wishes* may be
seen to stand for the totality of Johnson's writings as they
appear—or do not appear—in the *Life*. For what Boswell's
discussion, his quotation and commentary, excludes is precisely the terrible possibility that those writings carry within
them the seeds of their own deconstruction, that the magisterial philosopher and sage is nothing more than a soul

close to despair, vainly attempting to shore against the ruins of his age some fragments of classical wisdom and Christian theology, exploded systems of coherence and belief. To view the moralist in this light is to see him not as an Augustan survivor but as a lonely anachronism, and to see his outworn assumptions as the discarded lenses through which he futilely tries to impose order on a meaningless flux.

To view Johnson's writings in this light is to understand why that other Johnson, the uncouth denizen of the drawing room, appears as a moral hero to those who venerate him. For it is not that Boswell and Burke and Reynolds and the rest have been duped by their veneration of an idealized moralist into a veneration of the actual Johnson who produced the writings, but that the actual Johnson admits in his own life all those dark possibilities that the writings seem to exclude, lives constantly with the fear that existence is meaningless and the universe mindless, and through a gigantic and sustained effort of will denies the haunting specter of what Boswell once calls an eternal necessity without design.

Yet this other Johnson is not the Johnson perceived by Boswell or Burke or Reynolds, and to explain why they see him as a moral hero is to explain precisely what their perceptions shut out or exclude. The uncouth philosopher they venerate is, as much as the disembodied moralist, a creation or construct, a creature of their own deepest anxieties. The Johnson they encounter in life is, so to speak, a moral hero with no context to explain his heroism, a champion battling invisible adversaries in an arena invisible to ordinary men (and this explains, quite as much as Johnson's heroism, the quixotic light in which he so often appears in the *Life*). Yet the arena and the adversaries are not really invisible; they are terrible to contemplate, and focusing solely on the figure of Johnson as hero is a means of denying their existence.

Every idealizing perception of Johnson in the *Life*, then,

is subjected to the antithetical pressures—a field of deconstructive force—existing in the space between the world of his moral writings and the gloomy antiworld revealed in the *Prayers and Meditations*. To see that the magisterial moralist of the writings is merely the reverse or positive image of the miserable supplicant of the *Prayers and Meditations* is to see that every conception of Johnson that lies between them, even as it seems to include the complexities of a heroism mingled with despair, is finally precarious and unstable, a conception that wavers and dissolves as we move inward toward the center of the *Life*. And this is true not simply of Boswell and Reynolds and Langton and Burke, but of every member of that circle of veneration that composes the inner sphere of the *Life*.

To see why this is so, it is not necessary to trace in tedious detail the system of antithetical relations that works toward the dissolution or deconstruction of every idealizing perception of Johnson. For what occurs is that the system in its entirety, the *Life* as a whole, insists strongly on the dark possibilities that such perceptions exclude. Thus we see Johnson's melancholy, for instance, not as an occasional illness or disease, but as the retreat of a heroic spirit from the specter of a meaningless universe, a mode of spiritual paralysis:

> He was so ill, as, notwithstanding his remarkable love of company, to be entirely averse to society, the most fatal symptom of that malady. Dr. Adams told me, that, as an old friend, he was admitted to visit him, and that he found him in a deplorable state, sighing, groaning, talking to himself, and restlessly walking from room to room. He then used this emphatical expression of the misery which he felt: 'I would consent to have a limb amputated to recover my spirits.' (I.483)

When we attempt to explain the meaning of any such scene as this in terms of our conventional model of narrative structure, our impulse is to focus on its complication of perspectives; there is Johnson, living in solitary misery, there is Adams, entering the scene and reporting it later to Boswell, and finally there is Boswell himself, absent at the time but recreating the scene in his imagination in vivid detail ("sighing, groaning, talking to himself") before our eyes. Yet what cuts through all questions of mediation and narrative time is the shared perspective of Adams and Boswell, the perspective of a world that sees any such episode as this as "illness," as a "hypochondraick disorder," as a gloomy interlude in an existence altogether more cheerful and serene.

The *Life* as a whole, on the other hand, insists on an opposite reality, a reality in which Johnson's moments of serenity, even, in company, of hilarity and high glee, are momentary escapes from the despair that makes existence misery. Thus Johnson's lethargy, so often preventing him from exertion for months at a time, must, like his melancholy, be seen as a form of spiritual paralysis inexorably drawing us inward through the middle sphere of idealizing perceptions to the central reality revealed in the *Prayers and Meditations*—"my time has been unprofitably spent, and seems as a dream that has left nothing behind." And thus Johnson's horror at the thought of death, always seen by those who venerate him in terms of orthodox doubts about salvation and damnation, must be seen as a horror of death as mere annihilation; " 'when he dies,' " says Johnson of Hume's pagan stoicism in the face of death, " 'he at least gives up all he has' " (II.106).

To one degree or another, the consciousness of every inhabitant of the *Life* who perceives Johnson as a moral hero is defined by a denial of the dark and troubled reality revealed in the *Prayers and Meditations*—and this precisely reenacts, on the ordinary level, Johnson's own heroic attempt to deny the terrible reality of a blank material universe. The most prominent example in the *Life*, simply because the world of his consciousness is so prominent among the worlds composing its structure, is Boswell. In any scene where he turns to Johnson for spiritual reassurance in the midst of his own deep anxieties, the impulse to create or construct a Johnson answering his private needs is overwhelmingly visible:

> I said, I had reason to believe that the thought of annihilation gave Hume no pain. JOHNSON. 'It was not so, Sir. He had a vanity in being thought easy. It is more probable that he should assume an appearance of ease, than that so very improbable a thing should be, as a man not afraid of going (as, in spite of his delusive theory, he cannot be sure but he may go,) into an unknown state, and not being uneasy at leaving all he knew. And you are to consider, that upon his own principle of annihilation he had no motive to speak the truth.' (III.153)

The outlines of the spiritual dilemma that moves Boswell to introduce the notion of death as annihilation are visible here as well. On the one side there is Hume, symbolizing the world of Enlightenment skepticism, a world at once powerfully destructive of traditional ideas of order and cheerfully stoical in its pagan acceptance of a universe blind to the existence of men. On the other side there is Johnson, a spokesman for traditional systems of belief so powerful that he can for a moment dispel the dark clouds of doubt that surround Hume's cheerful behavior on the deathbed. And poised between them, in the doubtful position of every ordinary soul unable to sustain his own convictions without external support, is Boswell. Though the reassurance he receives can never be more than partial, it is reassurance nonetheless; "I thought, that the gloom of uncertainty in solemn religious speculation, being mingled with hope, was yet more consolatory than the emptiness of infidelity" (III.154).

The sense of reassurance derives, in all such scenes as this, from an utter denial of the possibility that Johnson's horror of death and Hume's pagan stoicism may be opposite reactions to an identical perception of the universe, that it is the notion of annihilation, so undismaying to Hume, that haunts Johnson's darkest dreams, lies at the source of his lethargy and melancholy, and oppresses his every waking hour. To see Johnson's unrelievedly gloomy view of human existence as having its source only in "the gloom of uncertainty in solemn religious speculation" is to locate him once again in the Augustinian tradition, to see him in all his private misery as a heroic defender of belief in an age of doubt, a spirit offering sustenance to lesser souls beset with fears.

To conceive of Johnson in this way, to create or construct a Johnson answering to the needs of a personal dilemma, is not, as it were, to operate in a void. For there is ample evidence—if one sees selectively, and denial now is nothing other than creation through a selective screening of elements—that some such Johnson exists. Now it is not only Johnson's moral writings but his speech, giving an unmediated view of a mind wholly committed to a vision of order and meaning in the universe, that seems to sustain the reassuring image. Johnson arguing with an overwhelming wit and energy and inventiveness for coherence and belief, as when in the scene above he instantly turns the argument of Hume's essay on miracles against Hume's own infidelity, always creates a powerful illusion of certitude in the midst of doubt.

Yet speech, precisely because it is unmediated, may always expose the illusion, threaten or subvert or deny the unreality one constructs. Thus there is another sort of scene in the *Life* that always works to subvert Boswell's perception of Johnson as an unfailing source of spiritual reassurance, a type of scene in which the Johnson of the *Prayers and Meditations* lurks gloomily behind the heroic spokesman for order and meaning:

I told him that David Hume said to me, he was no more uneasy to think he should *not be* after this life, than that he *had not been* before he began to exist. JOHNSON. 'Sir, if he really thinks so, his perceptions are disturbed; he is mad: if he does not think so, he lies. He may tell you, he holds his finger in the flame of a candle, without feeling pain; would you believe him? When he dies, he at least gives up all he has.' . . . BOSWELL. 'But may we not fortify our minds for the approach of death?'—Here I am sensible I was in the wrong, to bring before his view what he ever looked upon with horrour; for although when in a celestial frame, in his 'Vanity of human Wishes,' he has supposed death to be 'kind Nature's signal for retreat,' from this state of being to 'a happier seat,' his thoughts upon this aweful change were in general full of dismal apprehensions. . . . To my question, whether we might not fortify our minds for the approach of death, he answered, in a passion, 'No, Sir, let it alone. It matters not how a man dies, but how he lives. The act of dying is not of importance, it lasts so short a time.' He added, (with an earnest look,) 'A man knows it must be so, and submits. It will do him no good to whine.' (II.106-7)

At any such moment, the precariousness and instability of Boswell's perception of Johnson, its tendency to waver and dissolve under the antithetical pressures of the text, reveals itself in unmistakable terms. What is dissolving just at the moment is Boswell's attempt to see in an identical focus two utterly opposing Johnsons, the disembodied moralist of *The Vanity of Human Wishes*, in whose "celestial frame" is so great a source of spiritual reassurance, and the gloomy Johnson of the *Prayers and Meditations*, whose thoughts on his own death are so "full of dismal apprehensions." The model Boswell attempts to impose on the antithesis, that of a single mind subject to change of mood, is wholly inadequate to the occasion, and the scene itself dissolves in an angry rupture; "he was so provoked, that he said, 'Give us no more of this;' . . . and when I was going away, called to me sternly, 'Don't let us meet to-morrow' " (I.107).

By the antithetical pressures of the text, then, I mean precisely those pressures that at this moment undermine, subvert, and finally dissolve Boswell's idealizing perception of Johnson. For to say that Boswell attempts to see two radically opposing Johnsons in an identical focus is not ourselves to assert an opposition as unstable as Boswell's unstable perception of an unreal identity. It is the text itself that asserts that *The Vanity of Human Wishes* repre-sents one world—the ultimately serene world of the ideal-ized moralist—the *Prayers and Meditations* another, and the unmediated world of Johnson's speech yet a third, all in antithetical relation to one another. It asserts this through its discontinuities, its obeying of the laws of quo-tation and narration and dramatic or dialogue form; and in the moment we recognize this assertion we see Boswell's perception of Johnson begin to dissolve.

Antithetical pressures are at work as well within the sphere of idealizing perceptions of Johnson, the sphere of Burke, Reynolds, Goldsmith, Langton, and other members of the inner circle. For every such perception dwells within a separate world of consciousness, and every such world exists in antithetical relation to every other in the *Life*. Thus Boswell, after giving it as his opinion that Johnson's ludicrous convulsions are "of the nature of that distemper called St. Vitus's Dance" (that is, that they are merely physical in origin), introduces the opposing opinion of Sir Joshua Reynolds: " 'Those motions or tricks of Dr. Johnson are improperly called convulsions. . . . my opinion is, that it proceeded from a habit which he had indulged himself in, of accompanying his thoughts with certain untoward actions, and those actions always appeared to me as if they were meant to reprobate some part of his past conduct. Whenever he was not engaged in conversation, such thoughts were sure to rush into his mind' " (I.144).

Once again, it is the discontinuity of the narrative, signaled by quotation marks and textual space, that reminds us that Boswell's perception of Johnson, and Reynolds's, exist in the relation of world to antiworld. For it is not simply that Boswell's impulse to explain Johnson's convulsions as a physical disorder follows just the same pattern as his impulse to explain Johnson's private misery as an illness or hypochondriac disorder, or that Sir Joshua's explanation is less idealizing as at least allowing for a darker explanation of Johnson's misery, but that the instability of Boswell's entire conception of Johnson is revealed in the moment that Reynolds gestures, however indirectly, toward the gloomy world of the *Prayers and Meditations*. Yet Reynolds's own conception of Johnson, as denying in its own way the awful reality of that world, is in its turn unstable.

Throughout the *Life*, whenever we encounter one or another of the secondary accounts of Johnson interpolated in the text, our usual model of narrative structure invites us to speak of a multiplication of perspectives, of different angles of perception converging on an identical object. Yet all such accounts (and now Boswell's own narration figures simply as an account of Johnson occupying more space than the others) exist in the same relation to one another as does Boswell's to Reynolds's in this instance, as separate worlds of consciousness in a system of antiworlds. Whether it is the voice of Reynolds we hear, or of Langton or Beauclerk or Campbell or Boswell himself, each threatens the dissolution of all the others.

Yet our sense that we have passed through an intermediate space when we pass through the sphere of idealizing perceptions to the realm of the *Prayers and Meditations* is explained, as we have seen, by a logic of structure that locates these perceptions between the outer periphery occupied by the world of Johnson's moral writings and the central world of the *Prayers and Meditations*. The inner periphery, in a manner of speaking the last point of arrest

91

before we reach the center of the *Life*, is occupied by Johnson's letters and letters to him, an epistolary narrative with no plot beyond the transactions of separate minds in the world. Like a self-contained narrative in epistolary form, like *Clarissa* or *Humphrey Clinker* without the telos of events we call plot, letters in the *Life* embody a separate world.

To speak of an epistolary world within the *Life* is to raise just the sort of problem we encounter in epistolary fiction. For what seems to be a stable structure—consciousness speaking to consciousness through the medium of written language—is in fact radically unstable. Just as Boswell or Dr. Dodd or Mrs. Thrale address their letters not to Johnson but to their own conceptions of Johnson, all enclosed within a dialogue of their own making, Johnson addresses a world of imaginary correspondents, not Boswell or Mrs. Thrale but the Boswell or Mrs. Thrale he imagines to exist. The epistolary world contained within the *Life* does not dissolve but implodes upon itself, leaving us to gaze directly into the world revealed in the *Prayers and Meditations*.

The world of the *Prayers and Meditations* takes as its center the helpless cry of the supplicant on the dark edge of despair. Around this center revolve meditation and prayer in various other forms: prayer, for instance, as occasional utterance, as when Johnson prays before beginning the study of law or going into politics with H—; prayer as resolution, as in Johnson's endless schemes to regulate his life; prayer as self-examination, as in his annual review, usually during the Easter season, of the past year of his life. Through all this there are what Boswell calls "intervals of quiet, composure, and gladness," and in such intervals the gloomy center is obscured to our view. Yet there is a more powerful reason why that center is so often obscure.

Though one can explain the *Prayers and Meditations* only as a separate world within the *Life*, as one world among others in a vast system of antithetical relations, there is a sense in which the *Life* as a whole works to reject, almost as an organism rejects tissue it recognizes as foreign, the world they reveal. This is why, for instance, Boswell so often quotes only a phrase or so from those prayers expressing a naked sense of misery or despair ("in 1777, it appears from his 'Prayers and Meditations,' that Johnson suffered much from a mind 'unsettled and perplexed'" [III.98]) or so often buries in a footnote, at a safe textual distance from the main narrative, some dark hint of Johnson's private suffering. It is also the reason that the space occupied by the *Prayers and Meditations* in the text is so often given over to prayer as occasional utterance, as self-examination, as resolution to better regulate life.

When we perceive the helpless cry of the supplicant as the center of this world, then, we are tempted to say that it is the sheer intensity of Johnson's anguish that overwhelms everything else, cuts through all calm meditation and sober resolution to expose a naked center: *"'Have mercy upon me, O GOD, have mercy upon me; years and infirmities oppress me, terrour and anxiety beset me. Have mercy upon me, my Creator and my Judge'"* (III.99, italics mine). In such moments we perceive beyond all else a wasteland of the spirit, for this is not prayer but what Tennyson calls an agony of lamentation, "like a wind that shrills / All night in a waste land, where no one comes, / Or hath come, since the making of the world." Yet for all its intensity, its terrible agony of spirit, this is not why the helpless cry occupies the center of the *Prayers and Meditations*, the *Prayers and Meditations* the center of the *Life* as a whole.

The reason we seek is found, rather, in the nature of prayer itself, in the principle of supplication which, as Kenneth Burke has said, is "the most radically grounded aspect of language as a communicative medium." In prayer, says Burke, we "confront the making of two Absolutes: the cry *ab intra*, the solace *ab extra*. And what are the nearest, most *immediately personal* grammatical substitutes for that relationship? Obviously, an 'I' and a 'Thou.' "[3] The brilliant compression of Burke's remarks on prayer may be seen to expand into an entire explanation of the structure of the *Life*, not simply of the *Prayers and Meditations* as the center of that structure, but of the logic governing the series of deconstructions that draws us through a succession of dissolving worlds to the last reality they expose.

The *Prayers and Meditations* lie at the center of the *Life* because they contain within them the double nature of supplication. There is nothing double about the cry *ab intra* (" 'years and infirmities oppress me, terrour and anxiety beset me' "), for the meaning of Johnson's private misery lies precisely in the consciousness of his own mind or soul, an "I" seeking to complete itself in communion with a transcendent Thou. Yet we understand the cry *ad extra* (" 'Have mercy upon me, my Creator and my Judge' ") only when we see its doubleness, hear that it is not only a prayer to God but a prayer that there be a God to whom to pray. To pray that there *be* a God, a Creator and a Judge, is to have nothing to which to pray, and the terror of the cry *ad extra* is then that it becomes a cry into the blankness of the void.

The *Prayers and Meditations* are able to function as the center of the *Life*, then, only because the *Life* as a whole acknowledges only the first dimension of prayer, what Johnson expresses *in* speech when speaking directly to his Creator. What the *Life* utterly denies is the other dimension deriving from the nature of prayer as symbolic action, the cry *ad extra* revealing through the very form of supplication its radically grounded need to complete itself in transcendent communion. Yet the *Prayers and Meditations* embody both modes of signification, and it is because the meaning of prayer as symbolic action cannot ultimately be denied that it remains to haunt the *Life* as a dark dream

[3] Kenneth Burke, "Post-Poesque Derivation of a Terministic Cluster," *Critical Inquiry*, 4 (Winter 1977), 215-16.

of blank meaninglessness, a wind that shrills all night in a wasteland where no one comes.

Even to speak of the *Prayers and Meditations* as lying at the center of the *Life* is to return in a new way to the problem of presence and absence from which we began. For the very notion of a center now implies a notion of presence: if the *Prayers and Meditations* function as the center of the *Life*, it will be because there corresponds to them—exists behind them, so to speak, in the way that a person exists as a presence behind his speech—a Johnson somehow more real than all those Johnsons dwelling as idealized conceptions in the consciousness of others. Should there be, behind the *Prayers and Meditations*, not presence but an absence that they do no more than define, the very notion of a center itself dissolves, and we gaze into the *Life* as into a centerless structure, a system of purely antithetical relations in which every world is defined as a world by every other.

As a literary structure, however, the *Life* exists on just these terms. As much as Johnson's writings or his letters or his speech, the *Prayers and Meditations* are only a system of language or discourse, and behind them there exists no Johnson more or less real than any other—behind them there exists, quite simply, nothing at all. Yet the absence they define is not the same as that defined by Johnson's writings or his letters or his speech, and the question that ultimately demands an answer is how an illusion of presence, of a Johnson more real than any other, ended by drawing us to a nonexistent center, a world of private discourse to which nothing and no one corresponds. The notion of a vacuum at the center of the *Life* remains to tease us even when the notion of a center has dissolved.

The answer may be seen to lie in an alternative notion of what constitutes a center—that is, in something like Derrida's notion of a center as what we arbitrarily posit in order to make sense of an otherwise incomprehensible sys-

95

tem of elements. The center once posited, organizing and bringing into fixed relations the elements of an otherwise centerless system, the problem of unintelligibility or incomprehension is solved; the relations we seek to explain are suddenly there, and nothing remains but to explore them. The illusion of a Johnsonian presence behind the *Life*, and the logic of deconstruction that draws us toward the *Prayers and Meditations* as toward a center, can ultimately be explained in these terms alone.

The notion of an outer periphery or foreground in the *Life* begins precisely in an illusion of presence. The invisible monarchy of Courtenay's poem, the disembodied moralist who draws Boswell and Reynolds and Langton into the presence of an "actual" Johnson, are illusions in just the same sense as the notion of a Johnsonian presence behind the *Prayers and Meditations* is an illusion. To say that Boswell's idealizing perception of Johnson as a moralist dissolves in the light of antithetical relation, then, is nothing other than to say that we recognize the illusion as an illusion: the serene and elevated moralist he carries in his mind when he comes down from Edinburgh to London in his twenty-second year exists only because, to understand Johnson's writings as a world of discourse, he has had to supply a presence behind them, to posit an arbitrary center that is not there.

As with Boswell's narration, the separate world of his consciousness, so with every other world in the *Life*. The logic of deconstruction that draws us inward toward the *Prayers and Meditations*, through Boswell's account of Johnson and secondary accounts, through the world represented in Johnson's writings and the world of his speech or conversation, through the epistolary world of Johnson's letters and letters to him, demands at every stage that we recognize the illusion of presence as an illusion, that we see absence where a Boswell or a Reynolds or a Burke has imagined a presence. When we arrive at the *Prayers and Meditations*, at that unmediated center at which the *Life* enacts the agony of an "I" seeking desperately to complete itself in transcendental communion with a Thou, the illusion of presence, never more powerful, remains no less an illusion.

To understand the illusion, however, to see that there is only absence where the text promises a Johnsonian presence lying outside or beyond itself, is ultimately to grasp the meaning of the *Life of Johnson*. For as a biographical narrative the *Life* undertakes an impossible task, to give to the world a Johnson not identical with itself, to "preserve" Johnson, as Boswell says, in its pages, to allow us to penetrate through its structure to a presence that cannot be contained in but only represented by language. To discover at the end of the *Life* that there is nothing but the *Life* itself, that the biographical presence is only absence, is to discover the impossibility of its undertaking.

The subject of the *Life of Johnson*, we have always wanted to say, is Samuel Johnson, and by this we have wanted to mean something uncomfortably like that imaginary presence who exists only in an absence defined by the *Life* as a whole. Our sense of discomfort disappears, perhaps, only when we see that the true subject of the *Life*, as of all biographies, is the impossibility of the biographical enterprise, not presence but the illusion of presence ultimately revealed as an illusion, the dilemma of narrative trying and failing to reach through to a world beyond itself. To say that the *Life* is the greatest of biographies is to say that it confronts this dilemma more directly, works through the impossibility of its task more completely, than any other.

FOUR

THE WORLD AS SPEECH

THE *Life of Johnson* is dominated by its great conversation scenes, those gatherings around table or fireplace in which Johnson holds forth with brilliant wit and inexhaustible inventiveness on topics large and small, topics ranging from the constitution of church and state to the good or evil of cardplaying, and including everything, or nearly everything, in between. The world of the *Life* is in one sense a world organized around conversation, everything else playing a subordinate role in relation to the central image of Johnson engaged in social talk. Yet the relation of the conversation scenes to the rest of the *Life*, the way in which they figure as a dominant element in its vast and complex structure, has always remained a puzzle.

To say that the conversation scenes dominate the world of the *Life* is in one sense to ponder their relation to its structure as a whole, for what we are attempting to account for is our awareness that those scenes seem to stand out, mysteriously self-contained, as islands in the narrative stream. And to explain why this is so is to do more than explain that they constitute a separate world within the *Life*—for that is true too, we have seen, of Johnson's writings and letters and the *Prayers and Meditations*, of Boswell's narration and the accounts of Reynolds and Langton and Maxwell and others, of everything we recognize as a discontinuous order of discourse in the *Life*. All these stand out in their discontinuous relation to the rest of the book, and yet they do not stand out in just the same way as the conversation scenes.

At the same time, it is something Johnson's speech has in common with his writings and letters and *Prayers and*

Meditations—and then, by extension, something the speech of others has in common with his speech—that seems to explain why we want to identify the conversation scenes in their totality as a separate and coherent world. In Johnson's talk, more perhaps than anywhere else in the *Life*, we are given an unmediated revelation of his mind and thought, and we are given this, moreover, in terms more immediate than elsewhere. Johnson's conversation, unpremeditated and formed within the shifting confines of an unfolding drama of mind, is more immediate than his writing in just the sense that speech itself is more immediate or spontaneous than writing; the writer controls his situation, and conversation is drama precisely because the speaker's situation controls him.

The agonistic or ludic dimension of the conversation scenes is explained in part by just this consideration: they show Johnson struggling for dominance in the world of speech, entering into conversation as into a contest for superiority, most often winning but sometimes losing, playing a highly serious game governed by a set of invisible rules. And the antagonist is in some ultimate sense not anyone in that evening's company but the situation itself, ungovernable, filled with unforeseeable twists and turns, shaped partly by the laws of logic and the rules of rhetoric but also partly by randomness or chance. To establish superiority of mind through conversation in the *Life* is to defeat not the opponents but the situation, to assert the dominance of wit and imagination over a stubborn social reality that continuously asserts its own force.

Yet it is not really the immediacy of speech, or even its unmediated character, that explains why the conversation scenes seem to stand out in the narrative stream of the *Life*, but a different form of the illusion of presence I discussed earlier. Throughout the *Life*, I said, the illusion occurs whenever we see someone seeking behind discourse or language a presence that is not there—the disembodied and idealized Johnson, once again, that Boswell or Reynolds or

Langton imagines to exist behind Johnson's writings before they meet the uncouth philosopher who inhabits another reality. Behind language or discourse there exists nothing at all, and we become prisoners of illusion only when we posit a presence partially revealed in or partially masked by (it does not matter which), but not identical with, discourse itself.

This is just the view of discourse that the conversation scenes seem so powerfully to challenge. If Boswell has made a certain kind of significant error in imagining behind Johnson's writings an idealized and disembodied presence, and if the error, endlessly repeated in the *Life*, is what allows us to see its structure as a system of antithetical relations, does not the error derive precisely from taking speech or conversation as a misleading analogue? As a presence behind my speech, if you and I are talking, you recognize me, and this is true almost no matter what we choose to mean by "me"—a purely abstract principle of identity, or perhaps the body that sits silent, listening attentively, when it is your turn to speak.

In some essential sense, this would seem to be precisely the reality enacted by the conversation scenes: Johnson is there, speaking or listening, nodding or gesturing or uttering half-whistles or sudden ejaculations, and what the company sees, what is present to it, is the Johnson who exists as a presence behind his utterance. Yet in reality it is the conversation scenes that mount a powerful assault on the illusion of presence, that undermine and subvert the notion of presence we are least likely to see as being problematic, that reveal presence as a fiction that, once dissolved, leaves us only with the reality of discourse—and that, last of all, remind us of the mysterious significance of this reality precisely by dissolving the illusion.

The conversation scenes end by dissolving the illusion of presence, however, only because they begin by enacting it, and enacting it, moreover, in a certain significant way. The illusion as we encounter it throughout the biographical story is that the *Life* includes its imaginary audience in the conversation scenes, that the audience is present whenever Johnson speaks in just the same sense as Boswell is present, or Goldsmith, or any other member of that numerous company that surrounds Johnson in the typical scene in which he holds forth on the topic of the moment. Not physically present, of course—that is a sort of presence the *Life* finally regards as being trivial—but present within the sphere of consciousness registering and responding to Johnson's conversation.

The illusion is created by the unmediated nature of Johnson's speech: " 'Modern writers are the moons of literature; they shine with reflected light, with light borrowed from the ancients. Greece appears to me to be the fountain of knowledge; Rome of elegance' " (III.333). For when he speaks, when all mediating perspectives dissolve or are suspended, it is as though any distinction between those inside the scene and the invisible audience outside it is suddenly erased. It is not as though we were suddenly transported into the setting where Johnson speaks, though at first glance that is an attractive way of accounting for what I want to explain, but that Johnson's speech divides the world: there is Johnson speaking, and there are those who attend his speech, and we, along with Boswell or Goldsmith or Reynolds, are among the audience.

To say that the *Life* repeatedly erases the distinction between its audience and those present in the conversation scenes, however, is implicitly to ask wherein that distinction consists. In a world where we hear Johnson's conversation on just the same terms as it is heard by those in the drawing room he inhabits, become invisible members of the community of listeners, what grounds exist for saying that Boswell and Goldsmith and the others are inside the scene while we remain outside it? The answer that offers itself is, of course, physical presence: Boswell or Goldsmith see the Johnson who is speaking, but he exists for the audience of the *Life* only as an assumed presence behind his speech.

And this remains true even when Johnson's physical appearance is described: it is not a physical Johnson we see when Boswell describes his posture or his gestures, but a Johnson existing wholly in the language of Boswell's description, a figure created out of words.

Yet the structure of the *Life* simply disallows this sort of explanation: Johnson is physically present to those who actually surround him in the conversation scenes, of course, but his physical presence is only in a trivial sense what exists behind or corresponds to his speech. The body that sits in the chair is, like the chair itself or the table next to it, a material presence, something that belongs to a world alien to mind or soul or language. This is precisely what sustains the retrospective narration of the older Boswell who tells the biographical story: Johnson has gone to the grave, and the body that once inhabited those crowded scenes has begun to dissolve into dust, and yet the Johnson of the conversation scenes lives on in his speech, an endlessly vital presence.

Another sort of explanation is needed, then, to bring us closer to what is occurring in the conversation scenes, the sort of explanation we associate in other contexts with the notion of personal identity. For it is the principle of identity that organizes comprehension of speech as speech. The words I say to you at various times do not appear to you as unconnected or discontinuous fragments of language (though I may have said very different things about things very different) precisely because you posit as the source from which they emanate a single consciousness (which you may contingently see as being always accompanied by my body). My speech itself, my impassioned denunciation of the present government or my perfunctory remark on the weather, is not in itself either consistent or coherent; what makes it so is the center of consciousness you posit as existing behind my words, the presence or identity you call me.

The conversation scenes of the *Life* seem, after all, to

present us with an analogue of this situation. If Boswell and Goldsmith and the others recognize a single presence behind the discontinuities of Johnson's utterance, and if this presence, irreducible to the purely material body that inhabits the purely physical setting of drawing room or tavern, belongs to the realm of mind or spirit, then the presence they recognize is precisely that abstraction, that disembodied principle of pure identity, named Samuel Johnson. Thus we encounter, once again, the possibility of presence as illusion: is the abstract center of consciousness from which Johnson's speech emanates any less an arbitrary fiction than the idealized philosopher and sage Boswell or Reynolds imagined to exist behind the writings? In itself the question has only the general sort of interest it has in philosophical discussions of identity, intersubjectivity, and related problems. Here, however, it has a more specific interest, for it is precisely the question posed by the *Life* as a whole.

We understand the conversation scenes, that is, only when we understand that they reverse the perspective they seem at first to demand. It is not that the audience of the *Life* listens to Johnson as those present in the room listen to him, but that those present in the room listen to him as the audience of the *Life* does, continuously positing a single consciousness or identity as the center that organizes and brings into an order of coherence the radical discontinuities of Johnson's utterance. The inhabitants of the drawing room in which Johnson holds forth are in very much the same position as a reader of the *Life*, the position of having at every moment to construct a Johnson who corresponds to the discourse to which they listen. If the possibility that this is so never seems to occur to those present when Johnson speaks, it is only because the situation of the reader, puzzling over the problem of a presence behind the words he reads, reproduces in more radical form the situation the listener inhabits unawares.

Yet it is not quite right to say that no inhabitant of the

Life suspects that the illusion of a Johnsonian presence behind Johnson's speech is an illusion, an arbitrary center of coherence not present in the utterance itself but posited by the listener. The problem returns to puzzle Boswell, for instance, in the character of Johnson that closes the *Life*: "At different times, he seemed a different man, in some respects; not, however, in any great or essential article, upon which he had fully employed his mind, . . . but only in his manners, and in the display of argument and fancy in his talk" (IV.426). In his talk—the real subject of Boswell's puzzlement is not a superficial changeableness but a discourse too radically discontinuous to be reduced wholly to coherence by any one arbitrary fiction of presence.

The real significance of the conversation scenes, however, is not that they insist on all this; it is the way they insist on it that signifies. For the *Life* presents us with a world in which, when every illusion summoned up by language or discourse dissolves, we are left with language or discourse itself as the ultimate reality, a reality of mind or spirit in its eternal aspect. What remains when those who listened to Johnson's speech have disappeared, when the Johnson they saw before them and the Johnson they imagined to exist as a center of consciousness behind his speech have disappeared—what remains is Johnson's speech, that conversation that makes the *Life* itself permanent as a work in which everything else revolves around conversation, mind revealed not in but as language.

One reason that the conversation scenes seem to stand out as islands in the narrative stream of the *Life*, then, lies in their diametric reversal of the perspective we normally bring to narrative structure. To see those who listen to Johnson in such scenes, those sitting with him around the table or in the drawing room, as continuously constructing a Johnson who does not exist, positing a center of consciousness or identity that reduces to coherence the radical discontinuities of his discourse, is to see that the conversation scenes are themselves the primary model for the structure of the *Life* as a whole. In dissolving the illusion of presence in its most powerful and persistent form—the illusion that the speaker is present behind rather than in his speech—the conversation scenes expose a structure consisting in nothing other than its discontinuities.

There is, at the same time, a deeper level on which the conversation scenes operate as a primary model for the structure of the *Life*. For it is not only that they reveal the text in its discontinuities, or reveal the extraordinary lengths to which both the inhabitants and the audience of the *Life* go to dispel discontinuity through fictions of presence, but that they themselves represent a structure wholly antithetical, a structure with which we cannot come to terms except as a system of internal antitheses:

'I think (said Hicky,) gentility and morality are inseparable.' BOSWELL. 'By no means, Sir. The genteelest characters are often the most immoral. Does not Lord Chesterfield give precepts for uniting wickedness and the graces? A man, indeed, is not genteel when he gets drunk; but most vices may be committed very genteelly: a man may debauch his friend's wife genteelly: he may cheat at cards genteelly.' HICKY. 'I do not think *that* is genteel.' BOSWELL, 'Sir, it may not be like a gentleman, but it may be genteel.' JOHNSON. 'You are meaning two different things. One means exteriour grace; the other honour. It is certain that a man may be very immoral with exteriour grace. Lovelace, in "Clarissa," is a very genteel and a very wicked character. Tom Hervey, who died t'other day, though a vicious man, was one of the genteelest men that ever lived.' (II.340-41)

At any such moment, with the complete disappearance of anything we could call a mediating perspective, we gaze upon a world comprehensible only in terms of antithesis. As with drama, it is precisely an awareness of antithetical structure that organizes even our most conventional explanation of what is occurring: this is a world, we want to say, consisting of centers of consciousness in relation to other centers of consciousness, a network of intersubjectivity revealed in the form of dramatic dialogue. In such a world, where the otherness of the listener or listeners is a condition of speech, discourse emerges to give body or substance to the antithetical structure already invisibly present in the situation in that moment before the silence is broken by speech.

Yet our conventional explanations too derive from an illusion of presence—in this scene, the illusion that demands that we posit the silent presence of Davies and Hicky and Boswell in the moment of Johnson's speech, and posit, moreover, a Johnsonian presence behind and not identical with these remarks on honor and exterior grace. From our normal perspective, that is to say, the structure of the scene may be represented thus:

'   (said Hicky,)
    .' BOSWELL. '

.' HICKY. '

.' BOSWELL. '

.' JOHNSON. '

.'

Yet the structure of the *Life*, and the model of that structure revealed in the conversation scenes, demand once again that we reverse our normal perspective, see language as the

reality that remains when every illusion of presence has
dissolved, gaze upon discourse in its radical discontinuities
as the subject of the conversation scenes. The reality upon
which we gaze, then, always reveals itself in other terms:

'I think (,) gentility and morality are inseparable.'   . 'By no means, Sir. The genteelest characters are often the most immoral. Does not Lord Chesterfield give precepts for uniting wickedness and the
graces? A man, indeed, is not genteel when he gets
drunk; but most vices may be committed very genteelly:
a man may debauch his friend's wife genteelly: he may
cheat at cards genteelly.'   . 'I do not think *that* is
genteel.'   . 'Sir, it may not be like a gentleman,
but it may be genteel.'   . 'You are meaning two
different things. One means exteriour grace; the other
honour. It is certain that a man may be very immoral
with exteriour grace. Lovelace, in "Clarissa," is a very
genteel and a very wicked character. Tom Hervey, who
died t'other day, though a vicious man, was one of the
genteelest men that ever lived.'

Our tendency to see the names and attributive phrases—
" (said Hicky)," "BOSWELL," "JOHNSON"—as representing
the poles or boundaries of an intersubjective structure is
precisely a tendency to discover presence where there is
only language or discourse, to participate in the illusion
that the *Life* enacts in order to dispel. For these names are
themselves comprehensible only as elements in a larger
system of language or discourse—behind "BOSWELL" or
"HICKY" there lies not the real or substantial presence of
someone named but only absence—and the names themselves belong, like the quotation marks and footnotes and
textual spacings of the *Life*, to a grammar of discontinuity
that controls the text as a whole. The name that begins by
summoning an illusion of presence ends, inevitably, by
dispelling the illusion it invites.

At the same time, it is significant that the *Life* always does begin by summoning the illusions it ultimately dispels, by partially incorporating the models it repudiates. To see the conversation scenes as the primary model of the structure of the *Life* as a whole, for instance, is also to see that it powerfully invites the illusion of narrative continuity, of a biographical story steadily unfolding, that the scenes cast in dramatic dialogue undermine, subvert, and finally dissolve. If our sense of narrative continuity in the *Life* is exposed as a fiction, it is not after all a purely arbitrary fiction: it is the text itself that invites the model we vainly try to impose on its discontinuities.

To say that the conversation scenes work to expose on the level of narrative structure the same system of antithetical relations I have traced elsewhere in the *Life*, that is, is to recognize that the process always involves a movement toward rejection of some model or set of conventions, and that this movement is itself written into the text. If the *Life* as a whole summons an illusion of narrative continuity only to dispel it, it is because discontinuity has no meaning except in relation to some notion of continuity, as good has no meaning except in relation to evil, tallness no meaning except in relation to shortness. The structure of the *Life* emerges only when it has shown us what it is not.

The conversation scenes exist in relation to the rest of the *Life* as a world in relation to a system of antiworlds, then, only when we have failed in an attempt to reduce that system of antiworlds to order and coherence in the name of an illusory model of narrative continuity. And what emerges in the moment of our failure is a reversal of perspective, the possibility of a new model of narrative structure and a new vision of literary reality. This is the reversal we see in the most famous of the conversation scenes, the episode in which Boswell inveigles Johnson into a social encounter with his political and ideological adversary John Wilkes. Earlier we glanced at the Johnson-Wilkes episode; let us return now to trace the full process of reversal.

When we attempt to explain the Johnson-Wilkes encounter in light of a conventional model of narrative structure (precisely the model the *Life* invites us to impose on the discontinuities of the scene at its outset), we almost inevitably begin by explaining its structure in psychological terms—in terms, that is, of Boswell's own rising sense of expectation, his sense of near catastrophe, his sense of impending conflict when Johnson and Wilkes finally meet over the dinner table, and finally his sense of satisfaction in having contrived so dramatically satisfying an encounter. Those portions of the episode that actually consist of conversation, we want to say, are subordinate to Boswell's enclosing perception of events; they are contained within his mediating perspective.

The manner in which the scene invites this sort of explanation, obviously enough, is to dwell on the origin of the scheme in Boswell's consciousness: long before Johnson and Wilkes actually meet, after all, the idea of their meeting has formed one of Boswell's favorite fantasies. From this emerges the stratagem he employs to get Johnson to Dilly's table: "Notwithstanding the high veneration which I entertained for Dr. Johnson, I was sensible that he was sometimes a little actuated by the spirit of contradiction, and by means of that I hoped I should gain my point" (III.65-66). And gain his point he does:

JOHNSON. 'Sir, I am obliged to Mr. Dilly. I will wait upon him—' BOSWELL. 'Provided, Sir, I suppose, that the company which he is to have, is agreeable to you.' JOHNSON. 'What do you mean, Sir? What do you take me for? Do you think I am so ignorant of the world, as to imagine that I am to prescribe to a gentleman what company he is to have at his table?' BOSWELL. 'I beg your pardon, Sir, for wishing to prevent you from meeting people whom you might not like. Perhaps he may have some of what he calls his patriotick friends with him.' JOHNSON. 'Well, Sir, and what then? What care *I* for his *patriotick friends*? Poh!'

The illusion of narrative continuity is so powerful here that we can scarcely see, in the sudden shift from what we normally would call Boswell's mediating perspective to his dialogue with Johnson, the text dwelling on its own discontinuities. Yet this is what occurs, and in its occurrence we glimpse the beginning of that reversal demanded by the episode as a whole: the Boswell who stands retrospectively outside the action describing an earlier Boswell in whose mind the scheme was hatched, an episode conceived in the consciousness of a Boswell contained within the consciousness of a later Boswell, have simply disappeared. And within the separate world of dialogue, as within another sphere of reality, another Boswell suddenly appears.

In the intervening portion of the text, the suspenseful train of events that gets Johnson from his own house to Dilly's drawing room, the illusion of narrative continuity once again asserts itself powerfully. There is Boswell's dismay at finding a forgetful Johnson unprepared to dine away from home, the anxious consultation with Mrs. Williams, and finally, with Johnson's arrival at the scene, the discovery that Wilkes is among the company: "he had some difficulty to restrain himself, and taking up a book, sat down upon a window-seat and read, or at least kept his eye intently upon it for some time, till he composed himself. . . . But he no doubt recollected his having rated me for supposing that he could be at all disconcerted by any company, and he, therefore, resolutely set himself to behave quite as an easy man of the world."

At this moment, when Boswell approaches as nearly as he ever does in the *Life* to narrative omniscience, the illusion of continuity is overpowering. So overpowering, in fact, that unless we are extraordinarily attentive we will miss the countermovement that has all along begun to undermine the illusion. For interspersed throughout Boswell's account have been fragments of dialogue—" 'Frank, a clean shirt,' " " 'And who is the gentleman in lace?'—'Mr. Wilkes, Sir' "—that warn us of another reality taking shape, a

reality of discourse or utterance that will begin by crowding out and end by annihilating all impressions of continuity and mediating perspective, leaving us gazing into a
world consisting wholly of speech.

Yet it is our conventional model of narrative structure
that invites us to see conversation as crowding out or dis-
placing narration at this point: on a deeper level, what we
are seeing is a pattern of reversal demanded by all the conversation scenes in the *Life*. For what we understand when
we understand the reversal of our normal perspective is
that speech or discourse has been from the beginning the
primary reality, and the conversation scenes the primary
model of reality, in the world of the *Life* as a whole. It is
not that we move from one model to another, but that one
reality dissolves to reveal another—and further, that we
could have come to glimpse this new reality in no other
way.

Rather than say that conversation displaces narration in
the Johnson-Wilkes episode, then, let me say that Boswell
as a narrator or mediating presence simply dwindles or
shrinks to the point of invisibility, leaving a world in which
speech is the primary reality. When another Boswell reap-
pears within this world of speech, then, as when he inter-
venes to divert Johnson's otherwise inevitable explosion at
Wilkes's slighting reference to Garrick, it is as an actor or
speaker, a character existing on equal terms with everyone
else in the scene. Yet even now the reversal of perspective is
not complete; that occurs only when Boswell argues the
superiority of Scots law over English on the point of debtors
in meditatione fugae:

> WILKES. 'That, I should think, may be safely sworn of all
> the Scotch nation.' JOHNSON. (to Mr. Wilkes) 'You must
> know, Sir, I lately took my friend Boswell and shewed
> him genuine civilised life in an English provincial town.
> I turned him loose at Lichfield, my native city, that he
> might see for once real civility: for you know he lives

among savages in Scotland, and among rakes in London.'
WILKES. 'Except when he is with grave, sober, decent
people like you and me.' JOHNSON. (smiling) 'And we
ashamed of him.' (III.77)

Only when Boswell becomes an object of conversation,
in short, existing on equal terms with the absent Garrick
and the problem of interpreting Horace's *Ars Poetica*, do
we fully understand the implications of a movement that
carries us from a notion of conventional narration—Boswell as a mediating presence standing outside the scene and
describing it—to a world in which "my friend Boswell" is
reconstituted as an object of discourse. It is discourse about
Boswell that dissolves Boswell as a presence discoursing
about the episode, and that ultimately resolves the problem
of how he can seem to disappear from one sphere of reality
only to rematerialize, suddenly and disconcertingly, in
another.

The portions of the Johnson-Wilkes episode that consist
solely of conversation, insisting on structure as a system of
antithetical relations, have all along been subverting the
illusion of narrative continuity. It is not that Boswell, having dematerialized as a mediating presence, appears inside
the world of discourse, but that he has from the first been
a creature of a world of discourse radically discontinuous
in nature. The Boswell whose voice we hear telling the
biographical story exists on just the same terms as that
Boswell who sits at the table with Johnson and Wilkes,
and his narration is discontinuous in just the same sense
as is his speech within the conversation scenes.

At this point, perhaps, we can no longer tolerate what
Wittgenstein called the mental cramp that invariably de-
velops when our models of explanation do not answer to
the reality we are trying to explain. What is intolerable
now is the mental discomfort that arises when we try to
account for Boswell as a narrator standing outside the episode he is recounting. For if we perceive the conversation

scenes as the primary model of the structure of the *Life*, we
see that such a view can only commit us to a certain kind
of nonsense—as though, for instance, we were to try to
describe Johnson as existing "outside" Wilkes as he addresses him across the table, Wilkes existing "outside" Johnson when he responds.

Our sense of discomfort disappears only when we see
Boswell as a narrator existing in the same relation to the
biographical story as Johnson and Wilkes exist in relation
to each other in their conversation, and when we see further
that what we want to call the story itself dissolves into discontinuous worlds of discourse, into letters and diaries and
secondary accounts and footnotes—into the text of the *Life*
in all its radical discontinuities. For Boswell as biographical
narrator, like the Boswell who converses with Wilkes and
Johnson at the table, is a creature dwelling within the separate world of his consciousness, responding, reacting, describing, but never in his narration transcending—as the
illusion of the narrator as a mediating presence demands—
the world of his own discourse.

The illusion of narrative continuity that invites us to see
the conversation scenes as islands standing out in a narrative stream, the illusion so strongly insisted on by Boswell's
account of his own machinations in the Johnson-Wilkes
episode, is thus in a manner of speaking a necessary illusion.
Throughout the *Life*, it is a pattern of models partially in-
corporated and then dissolved that ultimately allows us to
see narrative structure as a system of internal antitheses, of
worlds in relation to antiworlds. The Johnson-Wilkes scene
merely illustrates in something like complete terms what
occurs whenever the text shifts suddenly from narration to
conversation, locating us once again in a world composed
of discourse alone.

Yet the conversation scenes, even as they reveal the antithetical nature of the narrative structure of the *Life*, simultaneously unveil a central element of its thematic structure
as well. For the thematic structure of the *Life*, on which its

meaning as a symbolic world depends, is determined by that system of antitheses that constitutes its narrative structure; and the same movement that dissolves the text into discontinuous orders of discourse, that subverts all conventional models and illusions of narrative continuity, yet insists on unity at a higher level of integration. Speech or language or discourse, though it exists only in its discontinuities, points toward a world of the logos in which speech or language or discourse is itself an ultimate and self-sufficient reality.

Throughout the conversation scenes, I have said, we see the inhabitants of Johnson's world imposing on his discourse a fiction of presence, constructing or inventing a single center of identity that, as the unchanging source of Johnson's speech, reduces to coherence its discontinuities. In relation to Johnson's conversation, once again, this invented presence corresponds to the idealized moralist and sage the world imagines to exist behind Johnson's writings; it is a magisterial Johnson, a heroic spirit dwelling in an age of spiritual crisis, whose voice they hear in conversation:

JOHNSON. '. . . No man now depends upon the Lord of a Manour, when he can send to another country, and fetch provisions. The shoe-black at the entry of my court does not depend on me. I can deprive him but of a penny a day, which he hopes somebody else will bring him; and that penny I must carry to another shoe-black, so the trade suffers nothing. I have explained, in my "Journey to the Hebrides," how gold and silver destroy feudal subordination. But, besides, there is a general relaxation of reverence. No son now depends upon his father as in former times. Paternity used to be considered as of itself a great thing, which had a right to many claims. That is, in general, reduced to very small bounds. My hope is, that as anarchy produces tyranny, this extreme relaxation will produce *freni strictio*.' (III.262)

Should it turn out that the Johnson whose voice we so often hear speaking thus is merely a fiction after all, a heroic presence conjured up by those who discover reassurance in his energetic utterance, his unwavering sense that a final principle of intelligibility underlies the confusion and disorder of human existence and human history, there is yet much in his conversation to support the illusion. For even when, as now, he is speaking in the gloomiest terms of his own age—"At last he burst forth, 'Subordination is sadly broken down in this age' "—his gloom has meaning only in reference to a vision of human society as it has sometimes existed and may again exist, of the universe as a divinely ordered reality and man as a creature who, in his best moments, transcends his own vice and folly and pride to become, in Johnson's vastly expanded sense of the term, a rational being.

In the same way, Johnson's remarks on even the most ordinary occurrences of the day display the same clairvoyance as his moral writings, the same power to penetrate the complicated surface of pride and folly to the unchanging reality of human nature underneath. The moralist who gave the world Dick Minim and a hundred other figures of harmless vanity is closely related to the conversationalist who, like Democritus in *The Vanity of Human Wishes*, always manages to pierce the human scene with a philosophic eye:

> Garrick added, with an appearance of grave recollection, 'If I were to begin life again, I think I should not play those low characters.' Upon which I observed, 'Sir, you would be in the wrong; for your great excellence is your variety of playing, your representing so well, characters so very different.' JOHNSON. 'Garrick, Sir, was not in earnest in what he said; for, to be sure, his peculiar excellence is his variety. . . . BOSWELL. 'Why then, Sir, did he talk so?' JOHNSON. 'Why, Sir, to make you answer as you did.'

BOSWELL. 'I don't know, Sir; he seemed to dip deep into his mind for the reflection.' JOHNSON. 'He had not far to dip, Sir: he had said the same thing, probably, twenty times before.' (III.35)

In his normal mode of conversation, Johnson the social talker seems to operate between the extremes of the idealized moralist and the laughing philosopher, moving from brilliant and impassioned discourse on serious matters to lighthearted pleasantry on vanity or folly, moving in a moment back again to seriousness, always following ideas to their level of ultimate implication. Within these extremes, which are closely related in terms of moral perspective, there does seem to exist a stable center of consciousness or identity, a Johnsonian presence revealing itself in changing but not finally in inconsistent ways. The illusion of presence or coherence in the conversation scenes, should it turn out to be an illusion after all, is obviously sustained by just this notion of a normal mode of Johnsonian discourse.

Yet that notion is itself an illusion, a fiction of coherence projected onto the discontinuities of Johnson's utterance. And it is only because Johnson's conversation does exist as a discontinuous order of discourse—can, as conversation, exist as nothing else—that the illusion becomes possible. The floating fragments of speech that can be brought into varying alignment with one another, arranged and rearranged to sustain various notions of Johnsonian presence behind utterance, are the materials from which are constructed the different Johnsons who dwell in the minds of Boswell, Reynolds, Garrick, Gibbon, and all the rest of those who inhabit the conversation scenes. The variety of conceptions that emerges whenever the physically absent Johnson himself becomes a topic of conversation in the *Life* reveals not a simple difference of opinion but a contest of related fictions of presence.

Though the sort of scene in which an absent Johnson is discussed by the company occurs throughout the *Life*, it is finally not by itself sufficient to dissolve the illusion of presence or coherence, of a stable center of Johnsonian consciousness that exists as the source of all discourse. For Boswell or Reynolds or Langton or Goldsmith, much as the imaginary Johnsons they construct from the conversation differ in outline and detail, seem at some essential level to agree in seeing a magisterial and heroic spirit behind the utterance; and against this background of shared perception any contrary conception of Johnson—Gibbon's, for instance, as he reveals it in an occasional ironic aside—seems merely to exist as a dissent. The illusion is dissolved, when it is dissolved, by Johnson's conversation itself.

Within the conversation scenes, that is, there are at work the same antithetical pressures that elsewhere in the *Life* draw us inward toward the world of the *Prayers and Meditations* only to reveal, instead of a last gloomy and suffering Johnsonian presence, a vacuum at the center of the *Life*. For the same discontinuities that allow the inhabitants of the *Life* to construct a Johnsonian presence behind the conversation ultimately threaten and dissolve every construction: to ignore the discontinuities of Johnson's utterance, to project onto it an arbitrary order of coherence external to itself, is to ignore or suppress everything inconsistent with the fiction, to banish beyond its circumference elements that, like gaseous molecules expelled from a vacuum, press inward on the space from which they have been expelled.

Like the idealized moralist whom Boswell and Langton and the others imagined to exist as a presence behind the writings, the magisterial conversationalist whom they imagine to exist behind Johnson's discourse is ultimately a figure serene in his vision of an intelligible order in existence. And so much of Johnson's discourse works to support the illusion that we are invited to see conversation in

the *Life* as a whole as an abstract arena within which Johnson combats, with all the brilliance of his wit, all the
energy of his endless inventiveness, a host of intellectual
adversaries representing the pride of what Burke calls, in
Reflections on the Revolution in France, naked metaphysical abstraction. From the drawing-room freethinker—" 'Sir,
I perceive you are a vile Whig' "—to Hume and Voltaire
and Rousseau, it is the more or less continuous presence of
such adversaries in the conversation scenes that creates the
image of Johnson as a moral champion surrounded on all
sides by the forces of spiritual disintegration.

On one level, then, the image of the magisterial conversationalist is undermined whenever Johnson is moved to an
angry outburst, cutting off conversation and signaling that
some chance remark has touched the nerve center of his
own deep spiritual anxiety. For it is always the Johnson of
the *Prayers and Meditations* whose voice we hear at such
moments, a haunted creature whose own horror at the specter of meaninglessness is the dark opposite of that magisterial speaker who dominates the conversation scenes; and
whenever we hear this voice, we are reminded that conversation in the *Life* is not after all an arena, but an escape
from that sphere of solitary suffering that lies behind the
outward conviviality of the drawing room and tavern.

Yet on a deeper level what works to dissolve the image
of Johnson as a moral champion speaking from unalterably
settled convictions, articulating a single vision of universal
order through all the variety of his scathing attacks on
freethinkers and philosophes, is the notion of conversation
itself as a ludic contest, a game of wit and intelligence
played according to a complex set of invisible rules.
Throughout the *Life*, these rules are raised to the level of
visibility whenever Johnson converses about conversation,
argues about argument; this is the context, for instance,
in which we glimpse the rule that discourse, to remain entirely ludic, must never touch on ultimate matters of faith
or belief:

Mr. Murray praised the ancient philosophers for the candour and good humour with which those of different sects disputed with each other. JOHNSON. '. . . They disputed with good humour upon their fanciful theories, because they were not interested in the truth of them: when a man has nothing to lose, he may be in good humour with his opponent. Accordingly you see in Lucian, the Epicurean, who argues only negatively, keeps his temper; the Stoick, who has something positive to preserve, grows angry. Being angry with one who controverts an opinion which you value, is a necessary consequence of the uneasiness which you feel. Every man who attacks my belief, diminishes in some degree my confidence in it, and therefore makes me uneasy. Those only who believed in Revelation have been angry at having their faith called in question; because they only had something upon which they could rest as matter of fact.' (III.10-11)

In the most general sense, Johnson's angry outbursts throughout the *Life* occur whenever one or another of the rules governing conversation as a game is broken. Thus, for instance, there are purely neutral rules having nothing to do with faith or belief—"JOHNSON. 'Sir, you put an end to all argument when you introduce your opponent himself. Have you no better manners? There is *your want*'" (II.-475)—as well as the rule that sets off conversation as game from the gloomy realm of Johnson's solitary suffering. Yet it is always the latter rule that explains Johnson's outburst when conversation takes a turn that touches his spiritual anxiety ("'I am angry with him who makes me uneasy'") and explains, too, why at such moments the image of Johnson as magisterial conversationalist begins to waver and dissolve.

When we look upon conversation in the *Life* as something always played within a set of invisible rules, on the other hand, we discover the principle that gives the conver-

119

sation scenes their own center of gravity, that allows them to figure in the *Life* as a world separate from other worlds. This is, once again, something that almost always emerges when we hear Johnson talking about conversation itself, as when he discusses Goldsmith's ill-success as a talker: " 'Sir, a game of jokes is composed partly of skill, partly of chance. A man may be beat at times by one who has not the tenth part of his wit. Now Goldsmith's putting himself against another, is like a man laying a hundred to one who cannot spare the hundred' " (II.231).

Yet the notion of conversation as a game of jokes represents a benign vision of social discourse in the *Life*, one that is belied even as Johnson uses the language of serious contest (" 'Goldsmith's putting himself against another' ") to describe the game. This is the more usual view of conversation in the *Life*; " 'that fellow calls forth all my powers.' " he once says when he has been seriously ill. " 'Were I to see Burke now, it would kill me.' " So much, observes Boswell, "was he accustomed to consider conversation as a contest, and such was his notion of Burke as an opponent" (II.450). It is the same agonistic notion of conversation that explains Johnson's approval of excluding undergraduates at Oxford from social intercourse in the common rooms:

> JOHNSON. 'They are in the right, Sir, for there can be no real conversation, no fair exertion of mind amongst them, if the young men are by; for a man who has a character does not choose to stake it in their presence.' BOSWELL. 'But, Sir, may there not be very good conversation without a contest for superiority?' JOHNSON. 'No animated conversation, Sir, for it cannot be but one or other will come off superiour. I do not mean that the victor must have the better of the argument, for he may take the weak side; but his superiority of parts and knowledge will necessarily appear. . . .' (II.443-44)

As a game, then, conversation may be entered in a spirit of deadly seriousness that yet does not deny its existence as a game. The child's total absorption in play, as Huizinga pointed out long ago, is due precisely to the nature of play as a sphere separate from ordinary existence, and the adult's absorption in a game of chess reveals the same truth. The ludic and the agonistic exist in the *Life* as different emphases on an identical reality; Johnson's exuberant wit and enormous inventiveness always reveal a seriousness not about the subject of conversation but about conversation itself, absorption in the game from which he so regularly emerges the uncontested victor.

It is the notion of seriousness about or absorption in the conversational game, in turn, that resolves the paradox of Johnson's antagonism toward the philosophes and freethinkers who, on the face of it, only practice in their writings the Johnsonian mode of talking for victory, arguing against received or conventional wisdom in order to display, through the sheer exercise of mind and wit, superiority of talents. Thus, for instance, Johnson's uneasy partial identification with the philosophes: " 'Rousseau, and all those who deal in paradoxes, are led away by a childish desire of novelty. When I was a boy, I used always to choose the wrong side of a debate, because most ingenious things, that is to say, most new things, could be said upon it' " (I.441).

Taken at face value, this is wholly disingenuous, for talking for victory in the *Life*, long after Johnson has entered his maturity, consists of choosing the wrong side of the debate and opening up a dramatic space in which wit and ingenuity can operate freely. If we hear the mature Johnson arguing most often against the opinions of the philosophes and freethinkers, it is merely because these have entered the body of fashionable, even conventional wisdom. He argues against them in just the same spirit as he argues throughout the *Life* against the assertion that luxury has corrupted the age, a sentiment tracing its antecedents back through the Augustan literature of his youth to classical poetry and ethics, precisely that body of tradi-

121

tional wisdom with which his admirers identify him. The issue is not the opinion itself but the ludic or agonistic context in which it occurs as an intellectual counter.

In drawing a distinction between himself and such philosophes as Rousseau, Johnson is testifying to his mature perception of social discourse as something purely game or contest. The error of the philosophes, like the error of Johnson in his youth, is an error of pride or egoism, the error of arguing against conventional wisdom and offering the unconventional results, supported by the wit or ingenuity of the argument, as a new kind of truth: " 'Hume, and other sceptical innovators, are vain men, and will gratify themselves at any expence. Truth will not afford sufficient food to their vanity; so they have betaken themselves to errour. Truth, Sir, is a cow that will yield such people no more milk, and so they are gone to milk the bull' " (I.444).

When we consider conversation purely as game or contest, on the other hand, the concepts of truth and error simply cease to apply—they are something that has meaning only in some sphere outside the game—and we have instead a notion of conversation as a realm wholly given over to the free play of mind or intelligence. Yet there is another sort of truth revealed in this notion, for in the *Life* mind or intelligence is identical with discourse itself; the truth of the conversation scenes is the truth of speech free from all constraints outside itself, and their protagonist is not some Johnson who exists behind his speech but Johnsonian speech in its own infinite variety and play.

The concept of disembodied discourse, discourse freed from external constraints and obeying its own invisible rules, is, of course, antithetical to any notion of presence, any perception of Johnson's conversation that seeks its significance in a mind or source outside or behind itself. Thus we see at work throughout the conversation scenes those antithetical pressures that dissolve the illusion of a Johnsonian presence behind the discontinuities of his social discourse, speech that, taken on its own terms as speech, ceaselessly undermines the fictions of coherence imposed on it from without:

> 'They make a rout about *universal* liberty, without considering that all that is to be valued, or indeed can be enjoyed by individuals, is *private* liberty. . . . Now, Sir, there is the liberty of the press, which you know is a constant topick. Suppose you and I and two hundred more were restrained from printing our thoughts: what then? What proportion would that restraint upon us bear to the private happiness of the nation?'

Then the world—in this case, as so often in the *Life*, taking Boswell as its representative—seeking to put back together the fragments of the shattered illusion:

> This mode of representing the inconveniencies of restraint as light and insignificant, was a kind of sophistry in which he delighted to indulge himself, in opposition to the extreme laxity for which it has been fashionable for too many to argue, when it is evident, upon reflection, that the very essence of government is restraint; and certain it is, that as government produces rational happiness, too much restraint is better than too little. But when restraint is unnecessary, and so close as to gall those who are subject to it, the people may and ought to remonstrate; and, if relief is not granted, to resist. Of this manly and spirited principle, no man was more convinced than Johnson himself. (II.60-61)

At any such moment as this, the attempt of Johnson's world to sustain the threatened illusion, to reduce to terms of "sophistry" those inconsistencies or discontinuities that escape the comfortable fiction of a magisterial presence behind the discourse, derives from yet another illusion. For Boswell's worried commentary, in turn sustained by our conventional notion of the narrator as a mediating presence, is only another order of discourse. The illusion of mediation occurs when we perceive his remarks merely as discourse taking discourse—Johnson's remarks on universal liberty—as its subject; it dissolves when we see that its true subject, the source of the anxiety we attribute to a nonexistent Boswell, is discourse as discourse, the puzzle of language in its discontinuities.

This is the puzzle that arises, with all its attendant anxieties and perplexities, whenever Johnson's conversation in the *Life* threatens to dissolve the comfortable illusion of Johnsonian presence that the world persists in discovering behind his speech. It is the puzzle that appears, for instance, as the problem of Johnson's roughness in conversation, the reduction of discontinuity to coherence always taking the form of the popular fiction of the crusty old gentleman with the heart of gold: "let me impress upon my readers a just and happy saying of my friend Goldsmith, who knew him well: 'Johnson, to be sure, has a roughness in his manner; but no man alive has a more tender heart. *He has nothing of the bear but his skin*'" (II.66).

In conventional terms, we should want to say that this explanation of Johnson's character, controlled by an archetype that reaches back to folklore, simply locates him in the tradition of literary benevolism, a tradition extending in the eighteenth century from Sir Roger de Coverley through Smollett's Matthew Bramble, and carried on into the nineteenth in such figures as Dickens's Mr. Grimwig. Yet to recognize this is at the same time to recognize that the model of character invoked by Goldsmith here, and by others countless times in the *Life*, is nothing other than a fiction of coherence, an attempt to project the traditional antithesis of rough manner and tender heart onto the discontinuities of Johnson's discourse, to impose order or pattern on an otherwise alien world of speech.

Yet the attempt to explain Johnson's character in these terms, to locate him comfortably within the contemporary tradition of literary benevolism, announces its status as a fiction of coherence at just the moment we notice its archetypal character. The tension between the Sir Roger de Coverley-Matthew Bramble character and the world of speech onto which it is projected, or rather the inadequacy of the model to the reality it attempts to reduce to coherence, is precisely what we are noticing. And the same is true of every fiction of coherence or presence we encounter in the *Life;* like Boswell's attempt to perceive Johnson as a magisterial figure who occasionally lapses into sophistry, all are finally inadequate to contain the reality they aim to reduce to coherence.

At the same time, it is the world of speech itself that attracts the inhabitants of the *Life* to Johnson, conversation in its ludic or agonistic aspect enacting the reality of discourse freed from all external constraints. If their need to discover a stable presence behind Johnson's conversation, to reduce its discontinuities to one or another order of coherence, testifies initially to a sense of anxiety or discomfort, it testifies at last to the power of attraction of that world that escapes explanation in terms external to itself. This is the context in which the *Life* becomes a work not about Johnson, but about, as Boswell once says, "the exuberant variety of his wisdom and wit" (I.421)—and in which the reaction of Johnson's world to his conversation is that of the anonymous gentleman "who being struck, or rather stunned by his voice and manner, when he was afterwards asked what he thought of him, answered, 'He's a tremendous companion'" (III.139).

It is never Johnson's voice and manner that are at issue in the conversation scenes, for those merely translate into terms of physical impressions the intellectual power of his speech. Those accustomed to Johnson's voice and manner, and so able to concentrate solely on his discourse, always focus directly on his speech itself. Thus we get, for instance, the typical scene in which Boswell arrives from Edinburgh and plunges immediately into conversation: "In a moment he was in a full glow of conversation, and I felt myself elevated as if brought into another state of being" (II.427).

And Boswell's impression on such occasions is the impression of Johnson's world as a whole: " 'I am now, intellectually,' " he exclaims to Mrs. Thrale, " '*Hermippus redivivus*, I am quite restored by him, by transfusion of *mind*.' "

To see the sense in which Johnson's discourse is the subject of the *Life*, I have said, we must perceive mind not as something expressed in language but as something identical with language. For the *Life* as a whole assumes an intellectual order stretching upward from the dumbness of the vegetable and animal creation through all orders of human discourse to a divine rationality implied by but finally lying at the outer limit of discourse—a world in which the logos exists as an invisible presence behind human society and in which human society dissolves or disappears to reappear as something manifest in language. This is the context in which the *Life*, as a text composed of discontinuous orders of discourse, comes to represent not only a world but, in an extended sense, its own subject.

Our sense of Johnson's conversation as dominating the *Life* might then be explained, we should expect, somewhat as follows. At the lowest boundary of the world of speech, just above the point where the brute creation leaves off and the human intelligence begins, we encounter the lowest level of human discourse—the level of savage societies, or, in civilized states, of the peasant or artisan. And in the *Life*, where social class figures as a metaphor for levels of intelligence, we indeed glimpse just this level; it is the level, for instance, of Johnson's old schoolfellow Mr. Jackson, "a low man, dull and untaught," who has fallen on ill times, having when Johnson meets him "some scheme of dressing leather in a better manner than common; to his indistinct account of which, Dr. Johnson listened with patient attention" (II.463).

The middle level of human discourse, we should similarly expect, is represented in the conversation of educated men and women in polite society. It is, in short, the normal world of the *Life*, a range of discourse represented both in the speech and the writing of those who move in Johnson's presence, in the accounts of Maxwell or Campbell as well as in the conversation of Goldsmith or Garrick or Mrs. Thrale. The chief representative of this level is Boswell himself, both the Boswell whose narration establishes a norm for discourse in the *Life* and that other Boswell who appears as a major figure in the conversation scenes, establishing by the normal tenor of his talk the distance between ordinary conversation and the exuberant wit and variety of Johnson's.

At the highest level, then, there should exist Johnson's conversation, continually reminding the listener in its brilliance and energy of that outer limit at which language becomes the embodiment of a mysterious principle of divine rationality present to some degree in every man but completely realized only in the supreme order of speech. This is the level at which we discover Johnson conversing in a manner that elevates his listeners as into another state of being, at which we continually see him dominating the company through the sheer power of his intelligence, at which men come out of his presence, as Boswell does, feeling as though they have been revived by a transfusion of mind.

Yet explanation in such terms as these, though it serves to account for much that occurs in the conversation scenes, leaves out that principle of ludic or agonistic contest that is a condition of discourse at the supreme level, that disburdens conversation of all purposes and frees it from all constraints external to itself, revealing a world consisting solely of discourse. It is not mind or intelligence that defines the supreme order of discourse in the *Life*, but that commitment to discourse as discourse that makes speech identical with mind: " 'There was (said he) no sparkle, no brilliancy in Fitzherbert; but I never knew a man who was so generally acceptable. He made everybody quite easy, overpowered nobody by the superiority of his talents, made no man think worse of himself by being his rival' " (III.148).

The notion of conversation *sub specie ludi* thus works to

exclude from the sphere of supreme discourse all those who, imprisoned within a system of social constraints or governed in their conversation by a sense of purpose beyond discourse, fail to understand the meaning of a commitment to speech or language itself, of a truth that cannot be contained in but must be enacted by discourse existing solely on its own terms. Whenever the *Life* ponders the puzzle of writers like Addison and Pope, capable of brilliant literary expression but wholly ordinary in social discourse, whenever it brings to light someone like Fitzherbert, talented enough to enter the conversational arena but restrained by a form of intellectual pusillanimity, we glimpse the standard of truth that explains Johnson's greatness as a conversationalist.

Within the conversation scenes, we see others who are capable of rising to the highest level of discourse—Burke, though as Johnson's great antagonist he figures most often as an unheard presence, occupied in Parliament giving speeches that " 'fill the town with wonder' " (II.16); Reynolds and other members of The Club, occasionally; and even Goldsmith in rare moments of inspiration and good luck. Yet it is always Johnson who defines the supreme level, the commitment to conversation as contest and discourse as mind, talking with an endless energy and brilliance that reduces everything external to discourse to the status of illusion:

'Sir, I would no more deprive a nobleman of his respect, than of his money. I consider myself as acting a part in the great system of society, and I do to others as I would have them to do to me. I would behave to a nobleman as I should expect he would behave to me, were I a nobleman and he Sam. Johnson. Sir, there is one Mrs. Macaulay in this town, a great republican. One day when I was at her house, I put on a very grave countenance, and said to her, "Madam, I am now become a convert to your way of thinking. I am convinced that all mankind are upon an equal footing; and to give you an unquestionable proof, Madam, that I am in earnest, here is a very sensible, civil, well-behaved fellow-citizen, your footman; I desire that he may be allowed to sit down and dine with us." I thus, Sir, shewed her the absurdity of the levelling doctrine. She has never liked me since. Sir, your levellers wish to level *down* as far as themselves; but they cannot bear levelling *up* to themselves. . . .' (I.447-48)

When we are absorbed into a world of speech in which speech becomes the world, everything else is an illusion: even if there was once a world of drawing room and tavern, of teacups and coffeespoons and speakers physically present around the table, all these have disappeared. Johnson, considered as a presence independent of his speech, has disappeared, and what remains in the *Life of Johnson*, a world of discourse revolving around the center of Johnson's conversation. This is the meaning of Boswell's insistence that his earlier *Tour to the Hebrides* is a work not about Johnson but about Johnson's speech, exhibiting "as striking a view of his powers in conversation, as his works do of his excellence in writing" (II.267)—an insistence that carries over to imply a view of the *Life* itself.

In the same way, the *Life* as a whole works to dissociate from Johnson's conversation everything external to its reality as discourse alone. Thus the remarkable moment in which a silent Johnson, having been shown some of Boswell's accounts of his talk, joins the circle of his own admirers: "as he had been used to imagine and say that he always laboured when he said a good thing—it delighted him, on a review, to find that his conversation teemed with point and imagery" (III.260). At just this moment, the Johnson who sits reading Boswell's pages, entranced not with himself but with discourse that will exist eternally apart from him, dwells no longer in his own world but within the world of readers of the *Life of Johnson*.

The conversation scenes are central to the thematic

structure of the *Life* not simply because they insist on a vision of language as mind, because they give us a world in which everything outside speech or discourse is refined out of existence, but because they bring into alignment the discontinuous modes of discourse of which the *Life* in its entirety is composed. When Johnson speaks, and when we understand that there is no Johnson speaking but only speech, every other element in the vast structure of the *Life* assumes its own relation to a luminous center where mind enters into language and, having passed through it into silence, leaves to eternity the world of its discourse.

FIVE

AUDIENCE AS ANTITHESIS

WHEN we begin by conceiving of the structure of the *Life of Johnson* as a system of internal antitheses, of worlds existing as such only in relation to a galaxy of antiworlds, we inevitably move toward an isolation of the textual logic that reveals illusions of center and presence as illusions. The same narrative or textual logic that so powerfully invites us to view the *Life* in terms of antithetical structure seems, moreover, to give us, whatever we may have thought before, a text radically unstable in its discontinuities. The stability of structure we saw before, this new perception of the *Life* invites us to say, was not written into the text but imposed on it from without. The puzzle of its structure was nothing other than the arbitrariness of that center of coherence that conventional interpretation attempted to project into a realm of pure antithesis.

Yet such a view only introduces a larger puzzle, the last with which the narrative and thematic structure of the *Life* confronts us. For even as we trace the network of antithetical relations embodied in the text, come to see the antithetical pressures under which various illusions of center and presence dissolve, we continue to speak of the *Life* as though it were a stable structure. And this, again, is not a matter of conventional models or paradigms through which we continue unconsciously to read, of arbitrary centers of coherence imposed from without. Rather, as with those other illusions, the illusion of stability is something written into the text, something that must be seen as an illusion before it dissolves.

The illusion of stability in an antithetical structure must derive, we may guess, from a grand antithesis or antitheti-

cal ratio that seems to bring into alignment the discontinuous orders of discourse of which the text is composed. In
the *Life*, we discover this antithetical ratio in the relation
between narrator and internal audience, between Boswell
and the imaginary readers to whom he tells the story of
Johnson's journey from birth to death. Even to speak of a
biographical story in the *Life*, of a continuous narrative
that threads its way through the discontinuities of quotation and conversation, letters and footnotes and secondary
accounts, is implicitly to isolate this ratio and the illusion
of stability it creates.

To conceive of the abstract relation between biographical
narrator and internal or imaginary audience as a controlling antithesis in the *Life* is to invoke a theory of audience
given its classic formulation some years ago by W. K.
Wimsatt: "In what is called the 'tone' of the poem, even the
most universalized audience has to be taken into account.
The actual reader is something like a reader over another
reader's shoulder; he reads through the dramatic reader,
the person to whom the full tone of the poem is addressed
in the fictional situation."[1] The view of audience implied
by Wimsatt's remarks, a view anticipated by Walker Gibson and recently reasserted by Walter Ong,[2] suggests a
theory of audience that was to remain undeveloped; in
contemporary literary theory, where the problem of audience has become a ground contested by rival claims, it is
rarely invoked.

Since it is the formal or objective view of audience, with
its strong suggestion of a controlling antithetical ratio, that
concerns me now, I need not pause to consider the newer
theories that have been asserted in recent years. Yet I may
note in passing that the reader response criticism of Norman Holland, the affective stylistics of Stanley Fish, and

[1] W. K. Wimsatt, *The Verbal Icon* (Lexington, Ky.: University of
Kentucky Press, 1954), p. xv.

[2] Walter J. Ong, "The Writer's Audience is Always a Fiction,"
Publications of the Modern Language Association (January 1975), 13.

various similar theories achieve what they achieve in the way of interpretive results only by ignoring the distinction between internal audience and actual audience. Thus Stanley Fish, whom we may in this context take to be speaking for subjective modes of interpretation generally:

> Perhaps, then, the word 'meaning' should also be discarded, since it carries with it the notion of message or point. The meaning of an utterance, I repeat, is its experience—all of it—and that experience is immediately compromised the moment you say anything about it. It follows, then, that we shouldn't try to analyze language at all. The human mind, however, seems unable to resist the impulse to investigate its own processes.[3]

In the contemporary conflict between objective and subjective modes of interpretation we may glimpse a larger conflict between two ideas of literature, one as an imaginative reality existing independent of the mind, the other as a Narcissus-mirror in which the mind of the reader discovers its own reflection. Yet the consequences for subjective interpretation of ignoring the presence of internal audience are grave, for it is just such an audience that we always encounter when we open the book and begin to read:

> Had we but world enough, and time,
> This coyness, lady, were no crime . . .

Here there are no questions about actual readers or ideal readers, objective readers or affective readers, but only about the imaginary audience the speaker directly addresses as *lady* in the second line of the poem.

To say that the *lady* of Marvell's poem is an internal or imaginary audience is at the same time to assert that, like the speaker who addresses her, she exists outside of time.

---

[3] Stanley E. Fish, *Self-Consuming Artifacts: The Experience of Seventeenth-Century Literature* (Berkeley: University of California Press, 1972), p. 425.

If "To His Coy Mistress" had by chance or mischance been hidden away in a drawer for three hundred years, its audience—the only audience that belongs to it as a purely literary reality—would have been the *lady* to whom the speaker addresses his utterance. The imaginary speaker and his imaginary listener, and between them the space occupied by language or utterance, represent the dramatic coordinates of an imagined world. To demonstrate that the same coordinates exist in every literary work—even in drama, where the world of the play projects an internal audience wholly distinct from any actual audience of readers or theatergoers—would be to develop just that theory of audience implied by Wimsatt's formulation.

To understand why that theory was never·developed, we need only glance at a certain theoretical weakness implicit in its formulation. For when Wimsatt describes the actual reader of a literary work as "a reader over another reader's shoulder," it is obvious that the term "reader" is doing a kind of illegitimate double duty; the point of Wimsatt's remarks is that the *lady* of "To His Coy Mistress" and any actual reader belong to utterly different spheres of reality, and to describe both as listeners or readers is only to surround an otherwise crucial insight with obscurity or outright confusion. The insight that is obscured is that no such thing as audience exists in literature, and that a genuine theory of audience would have to account for its nonexistence.

In any moment of objective comprehension, that is, the *lady* of "To His Coy Mistress" exists for any actual reader not as an audience but as an X. The source of confusion present when we describe the X as a listener or audience is again present, perhaps in clearer terms, when we describe the X as (say) a woman: "the internal audience of Marvell's 'To His Coy Mistress' is a woman." This is just the confusion that reveals itself when we attempt to transfer the term "woman" from its ordinary-language context (my sister will soon be a woman, I ran into a woman on the street yesterday, I pinched a woman on the arm and she screamed) to the *lady* of Marvell's poem: "the *lady* (of 'To His Coy Mistress') is a woman"; "I ran into the *lady* (of 'To His Coy Mistress') on the street yesterday"; "I pinched the *lady* (of 'To His Coy Mistress') on the arm and she screamed."

When we perceive Marvell's poem as belonging to a sphere of reality separate from the world of actual readers, it is clear that any such statement as "my mother, my sister, and the *lady* of 'To His Coy Mistress' are women" must have either the form "my mother, my sister, and X are women" or "X, Y, and the *lady* of 'To His Coy Mistress' are women." This is precisely what we mean, in fact, when we say that the poem, or any literary work, embodies a separate reality: when we are reading or discussing "To His Coy Mistress" it is the X we describe as a woman or a listener or an audience that is real, and the world we otherwise inhabit, the world of me, my mother, my sister, exists only as the unreal analogue of what is real.

The reason we speak of audience in literature at all may be explained in the same way. The X of Marvell's poem does not itself supply or even suggest any context in which it is to be explained; it is, in a manner of speaking, silent on the terms in which it is to be discussed, and in order to explain or discuss it we must borrow our terms by analogy from the only world we know—a world in which my mother and sister are identified as women, or in which actual audiences attend to the utterance of actual speakers. The significant point is that any term thus borrowed is purified by analogy, refined or disburdened of its associations in ordinary discourse. The term "audience" is in this respect rather like the coin we use to replace a missing chess piece: as long as the game continues, the penny on the board is not a penny but a pawn.

In speaking of audience in the *Life of Johnson*, we obey the same rule of analogy whenever we refer to the X as an imaginary group of readers addressed by Boswell as biographical narrator. Like the gentle reader so often addressed in direct terms by the narrator of *Tom Jones*, or that even more visible group of worships and reverences so frequently addressed in direct terms by Tristram Shandy, the internal audience of the *Life* is continuously in the eye of its narrator, and Boswell's consciousness of its presence goes far to explain his own self-consciousness as the teller of the biographical story. The special power of the audience projected by Boswell's narration is, as we shall see, the power to pass moral judgment on Johnson and the world that venerates him.

Yet the presence of an imaginary audience does not so far explain why, in relation to Boswell, it seems to provide a controlling antithetical ratio in the *Life*, or why there derives from this ratio an illusion of stable narrative structure. That illusion begins in the conventional notion of Boswell as a narrator who stands outside the world of the story, a mediating presence through whose perception of events we view the world inhabited by Johnson as biographical hero. Yet we have seen that this is itself an illusion, that Boswell dwells in the separate world of his own consciousness and that his narration is a discontinuous response to a story itself composed of discontinuous orders of discourse. From where, then, derives the illusion of narrative stability?

The answer lies in Boswell's role as the only speaker in the *Life* who addresses his discourse to an audience he conceives also to exist outside the story he is telling. This is really what we have in mind when, in a text so largely composed of secondary accounts of Johnson, we call Boswell a biographical narrator, and when we distinguish his discourse from that of others under the name of narration. It is the relation of a narrator outside the story speaking to an audience outside the story that brackets everything that occurs within the *Life*, creating simultaneously the idea of a controlling antithesis and that illusion of structural

136

stability that persists even when we are fully aware of the discontinuities of the text.

The reason we are led to speak of the relation between Boswell and his imaginary audience as an antithetical ratio lies, in turn, in the purely abstract nature of that relation as described by Wimsatt so many years ago. When we read Marvell's "To His Coy Mistress" with an awareness that neither speaker nor audience exists in any ordinary sense, that there is no lover or lady actually there in the poem, we suddenly see that we are dealing not with lovers and ladies but with the grand antithesis that is a condition of utterance itself, the subject-object or I-Thou relation that gives meaning to the notion of speech or discourse. An utterance that occurred outside the I-Thou context would be, if we could even imagine it to exist, not utterance but something else.

Yet this insight into the underlying structure of literary discourse, even as it invites us to conceive of the *lady* of Marvell's poem or the imaginary audience of the *Life* as an X or abstract outer limit of discourse, suggests why the presence of internal audience seems to confer on the *Life* an ultimate narrative stability. For the lover of the poem or Boswell as narrator of the *Life* cannot, after all, be viewed as addressing an abstract limit of discourse: the *lady* of "To His Coy Mistress" and the imaginary audience of the *Life* are what they are—what we describe as, respectively, a young woman and an imaginary body of readers—as a consequence of the subject-object relationship. This is why Marvell's poem becomes an absurdity if we conceive of its speaker as addressing an old man, the *Life* an absurdity if we imagine Boswell to be telling his story to a coy mistress.

Everything within the *Life*, then, is in fact bracketed within the enclosing antithesis represented in Boswell's relation to an imaginary audience; this is what we want to account for when we speak either of Boswell or of his audience as standing outside the story, Langton and Reynolds and Goldsmith and the rest as existing within its confines. The illusion of narrative stability in the *Life* is not, to this point, an illusion, and we encounter once again the principle that always occurs in the *Life* when such notions as center and presence and stability are revealed as illusions; the possibility is written into the text at the outset, and we understand it as illusion only when it comes to be denied, as a possibility, by the text itself.

The possibility of narrative stability in the *Life* is ultimately denied by Boswell's own existence as a narrator dwelling within the separate world of his own consciousness, by the existence of his imaginary audience as, after all, only an imaginary presence. For the audience Boswell addresses is imaginary not only in the abstract sense I have discussed, the sense that it corresponds to no actual audience or body of readers whatever, but also in the sense that it is projected by the *Life* as a presence already purely imaginary. It is not simply that Boswell's narration assumes the existence of an imaginary audience, but that so much of his narration shows him repeatedly imagining the audience to whom he addresses his remarks and asides, struggling to discover the presence of the readers who will pass judgment on Johnson and his circle.

This is the context, as we have seen, in which Boswell as a mediating presence dwindles to a solitary voice within the *Life*, the discontinuities of his narration revealing a distributed response to the other orders of discourse in the *Life*. It is within the same context that the imaginary audience of the *Life* dwindles to become only the abstract outer limit of Boswell's discontinuous narration, not the outer limit of a grand antithesis but only a condition of one order of discourse within the text. When we see that neither Boswell nor his imaginary audience exists except as they are projected by his narration, we arrive at the reality, the one reality on which the *Life* ultimately insists, of narration as discourse, discourse as language existing solely as language.

At the same time, the illusion of stability created by the controlling antithetical ratio implied by Boswell's relation to an audience outside the biographical story is so powerful, is itself so stable before it is finally denied as a possibility by the text, that it provides the means to explain why we must discuss so much in the *Life* as though it were a stable structure—why, for instance, we are able to speak of a division of the world of the *Life* into an inner and an outer sphere, or of an invisible law of moral gravitation that draws its inhabitants toward a Johnsonian center whose existence the text denies. All this belongs to the drama of Boswell's relation to an imaginary audience, and to the illusion that this relation brackets or encloses everything else within the world of the story.

To see why this is so, let us look again at that movement that carries us through a series of deconstructions from the idealized image that dominates the foreground of the *Life* to the gloomy center represented by the *Prayers and Meditations*. Even when that idealized image dissolved, I said, giving way to darker and more complex conceptions of Johnson as an actual presence, it in some sense remained to exert a force to the very end of the biographical story. And now we have a resolution of the paradox of its mysterious persistence: the idealized image dissolves under the antithetical pressures of the text, but it remains in Boswell's consciousness to control, throughout the *Life*, his relation to an imaginary audience. Here, once again, is the idealized Johnson of Courtenay's poem:

> 'By nature's gifts ordain'd mankind to rule,
> He, like a Titian, form'd his brilliant school;
> And taught congenial spirits to excel,
> While from his lips impressive wisdom fell.
>
> . . . . .
>
> Nor was his energy confin'd alone
> To friends around his philosophick throne;

Its influence wide improv'd our letter'd isle,
And lucid vigour mark'd the general style:
As Nile's proud waves, swoln from their oozy bed,
First o'er the neighbouring meads majestick spread;
Till gathering force, they more and more expand,
And with new virtue fertilise the land.'

As the biographical story unfolds, we saw, this image dissolves and there emerges the figure of an infinitely more complex and heroic Johnson whose moral wisdom is won through a constant struggle with despair, whose moral sanity is balanced by personal eccentricities too visible to be ignored, and whose moral penetration derives from his own sense of tragic self-deception. How then does the *Life* in the end suggest that there has been an essential truth in the image all along, that the idealized and disembodied perception of Johnson existing in the mind of the public, the "majestick teacher of moral and religious wisdom," as Boswell once calls him, is as real as the spiritual anxiety of the age that creates it?

The answer is that it is not the idealized image of Courtenay's poem that lingers in Boswell's consciousness as he tells the biographical story, but the metaphor of Johnson as an intellectual ruler of men, a magnetic presence who gathers a brilliant school of friends around his philosophic throne, whose majestic wisdom overflows to enrich an entire age. For long after the idealized image dissolves, the metaphor remains to control Boswell's perception of another Johnson and another world—that actual world of tavern and drawing room where Johnson is physically present to his company—and finally to control Boswell's perception of his own relation to the audience of the *Life*.

At the same time, the metaphor of Johnson as an intellectual monarch explains the division of the *Life* as a whole into an inner and an outer sphere. For now it is not simply that Boswell comes down from Edinburgh as a young man carrying in his mind an image of Johnson as a philosopher living in "a state of solemn elevated abstraction," or that this image begins to waver and dissolve in the moment the door of Johnson's Temple chambers opens to reveal an uncouth figure in rusty clothes and unpowdered wig, but that what survives the antithetical pressures of the moment is the notion of Boswell's penetration to the center of a moral world. In Johnson's presence, no matter what unexpected sights greet him there, he has entered the circle around a philosophic throne.

This is why, for instance, Boswell so strongly identifies his own authority as a biographical narrator with his penetration to and presence at an invisible center, why he so constantly reminds his imaginary readers that the Johnson of his biographical story is a figure they can know only through him: "I cannot too frequently request of my readers, while they peruse my account of Johnson's conversation, to endeavour to keep in mind his deliberate and strong utterance. His mode of speaking was indeed very impressive; and I wish it could be preserved as musick is written . . ." (II.326-27). This is not the simple authority of personal knowledge, of a biographer who knew his subject while his readers did not, for personal knowledge is not enough. Both Hawkins and Mrs. Piozzi, at whose accounts of Johnson Boswell directs scornful shafts throughout the *Life*, after all knew Johnson personally, and in Piozzi's case intimately. What they did not understand, and what cannot be understood by anyone who does not perceive Johnson as a moral hero, is the moral topography of Johnson's world.

When we see that Boswell's narration is controlled by a sense of moral topography, by a conception of Johnson as a moral center from which all else radiates outward, we immediately glimpse the invisible circumference of what I have called the inner world of the *Life*. Within this circumference move those who share Boswell's perception of Johnson as a moral hero, who understand his Toryism and his religious orthodoxy as an embattled fortress of faith in an age of spiritual doubt, and who hear in his conversation the sounds of an abstract and unending conflict with the forces of skepticism and unbelief. This is the moral community for which Boswell speaks when he describes the effect of Johnson's conversation on his own wavering spirit: "I complained of a wretched changefulness, so that I could not preserve, for any long continuance, the same views of any thing. It was most comfortable to me to experience, in Dr. Johnson's company, a relief from this uneasiness. His steady vigourous mind held firm before me those objects which my own feeble and tremulous imagination frequently presented, in such a wavering state, that my reason could not judge well of them" (III.193).

The same sense of moral topography, the same metaphor of Johnson as ruler over an invisible monarchy of mind and moral wisdom, determines the existence of an outer sphere in the world of the *Life*. For beyond the circumference of its inner world are those who do not, for one or another reason, share a perception of Johnson as a superior man. The most visible inhabitants of the outer sphere are the philosophes and their followers, all those who have mounted an assault on the foundations of traditional wisdom, morality, and belief. Since Boswell as narrator looks outward from the Johnsonian center, inhabitants of the outer sphere always appear as figures iniquitous or misled by a foolish vanity.

If Boswell's relation to an imaginary audience implies an idea of controlling antithesis, then, and if that relation is in turn controlled by Boswell's sense of moral topography in the *Life*, we see how the larger antithesis brings into alignment the discontinuous orders of discourse interwoven with Boswell's narration. In the conversation scenes, for instance, we repeatedly hear Johnson attacking the philosophes as vain men (" 'Truth will not afford sufficient food to their vanity; so they have betaken themselves to errour' ") or as simply malicious (" 'Rousseau, Sir, is a very bad man. I would sooner sign a sentence for his transportation, than that of any felon who has gone from the Old Bailey these many years' " [II.12]). The energy of Johnson's repudiation, though it belongs to a world separate from Boswell's narration, works powerfully to banish all philosophes and freethinkers to the outer sphere of the *Life*.

Yet the illusion of narrative stability at such moments, of an inner and outer world that exist not simply in Boswell's perception but in the *Life* as a whole, is sustained by more than this sort of alignment, by more than a set of narrative relations that seem to survive the antithetical pressures of the text. For as long as the *Life* insists on Boswell's relation to an audience outside the story, as long as we are aware of a grand antithesis that brackets everything else within the *Life*, the world of the *Life* is the world of Boswell's consciousness, and its moral topography seems to exist independent of his consciousness. This is why the *Life*, in all its discontinuities, from the perspective of a controlling antithesis seems to expand and stabilize Boswell's perception of Johnson and his world.

This is just the perspective from which so much of Johnson's discourse in the conversation scenes works to sustain the notion of an inner and outer sphere. Such adversaries as Hume, Rousseau, and Voltaire, whether they are truly malicious or simply vain, are too powerful to be dismissed peremptorily, and much of Johnson's conversation in the *Life* is devoted to defending traditional morality against their assault. This is the context in which the conversation scenes represent an arena of intellectual combat, with Johnson fighting a heroic rearguard action against the destructive skepticism of the Enlightenment. The measure of his superiority, and of the moral heroism that allows him to sustain a triumphant orthodoxy in a climate of spiritual disintegration, is that the rearguard action so often seems a victorious counteroffensive.

Whenever we see Johnson in this light, we are dealing no longer with his speech as discourse, as a ludic or agonistic contest that expands to include such abstract adversaries as

143

Hume, Voltaire, and Rousseau, but with a meaning discovered in his discourse by Boswell and all those whom Boswell conceives to inhabit the inner world of the *Life*. This is the explanation of that dominant image of Johnson arguing with such energy, wit, and inventiveness that his adversaries seem for the moment mere shadows without substance, as in the exchange on Hume's deathbed stoicism:

> I mentioned to Dr. Johnson, that David Hume's persisting in his infidelity, when he was dying, shocked me much. JOHNSON. 'Why should it shock you, Sir? Hume owned he had never read the New Testament with attention. Here then was a man, who had been at no pains to inquire into the truth of religion, and had continually turned his mind the other way. . . .' I said, I had reason to believe that the thought of annihilation gave Hume no pain. JOHNSON. 'It was not so, Sir. He had a vanity in being thought easy. It is more probable that he should assume an appearance of ease, than that so very improbable a thing should be, as a man not afraid of going (as, in spite of his delusive theory, he cannot be sure but he may go,) into an unknown state, and not being uneasy at leaving all he knew. And you are to consider, that upon his own principle of annihilation he had no motive to speak the truth.' (III.153)

The very power and energy of Johnson's utterance thus becomes, for Boswell and those who share his veneration of Johnson, a means of accommodating the melancholy and despair that otherwise seem so anomalous. For their impression of Johnson's superiority derives from a sense that his unyielding allegiance to traditional morality and orthodox belief has been won through an inward process of doubt that takes him to the edge of despair. Even as Boswell denies the possibility, and insists on treating Johnson's hypochondria as a mere disorder or illness, we come to perceive that the cost of the spiritual victory that allows Johnson to direct his own doubts into orthodox channels is the melancholy—the "dejection, gloom, and despair, which made existence misery"—that comes upon him when the illusion of certainty fails.

In the world of the *Life*, the truth of revelation and the wisdom of tradition have other adherents, from the complacent Dr. Adams ("DR. ADAMS. 'What do you mean by damned?' JOHNSON. (passionately and loudly) 'Sent to Hell, Sir, and punished everlastingly.' DR. ADAMS. 'I don't believe that doctrine' " [IV.299]) to the pious ladies who so often engage Johnson in religious conversation. What gives meaning to Johnson's combat with the forces of skepticism and unbelief in the eyes of those who venerate him is his own victory over (as he calls them in a prayer composed close to his death) inquisitive and perplexing thoughts, " 'difficulties vainly curious, and doubts impossible to be solved' " (IV.370). Johnson's power to reassure lesser souls, to banish the specter of a meaningless universe and maintain the reality of a comprehensible and divinely ordained order of things, is the power of one who has met the skepticism of the philosophes on its own ground, who has won victory over doubts far deeper than theirs.

The inner world of the *Life*, then, is inhabited not simply by those who share Boswell's perception of Johnson as a superior man, but by those who recognize his superiority specifically as a power of spiritual affirmation that has otherwise disappeared from their world. This is the great truth of Carlyle's famous description, in *Heroes and Hero-Worship*, on Johnson's relation to his age: "the Eighteenth was a *Sceptical* Century. . . . Scepticism means not intellectual doubt alone, but moral Doubt; all sorts of infidelity, insincerity, spiritual paralysis. Perhaps, in few centuries that one could specify, was a life of Heroism more difficult for a man. That was not an age of Faith,—an age of Heroes!" Carlyle, writing about the Johnson he found in the pages of the *Life*, speaks in effect as a member of the inner world of the biographical story. From minor characters to men as extraordinary as Reynolds or Burke, the inhabitants of that world discover in Johnson's presence a refuge not from intellectual but from moral doubt, from all sorts of infidelity, insincerity, spiritual paralysis.

The outer world of the *Life*, on the other hand, is populated not simply by the philosophes, freethinkers, and Whigs who figure in Johnson's conversation as abstract adversaries, but by all those who through laxity or triviality of spirit or simple complacency remain untroubled by matters of ultimate concern. The comedy of any such scene as Johnson's meeting with his old schoolfellow Mr. Edwards is in this sense a comedy of nonrecognition; such men as this rattle on undistractedly in Johnson's presence ("EDWARDS. 'You are a philosopher, Dr. Johnson. I have tried too in my time to be a philosopher; but, I don't know how, cheerfulness was always breaking in' " [III.305]) precisely because they correspond, in the world of the *Life*, to William James's once-born souls. Their failure to perceive Johnson as a superior man is a failure of moral or spiritual perception. Yet such souls are, in their superficiality and complacency, the unwitting allies of the philosophes and freethinkers, for they create the climate of laxity in which unbelief alone can flourish.

The philosophes, however, best symbolize the nature of the *Life*'s antagonistic outer world, for theirs is the moral and intellectual perspective that threatens to abolish the very ground on which Johnson stands as a hero. The passion with which Johnson attacks such men as Voltaire, Rousseau, and Hume would be met, we are always aware, not with an answering passion but with urbane mockery, with the ironic and superior detachment that is the freethinker's most powerful weapon not simply against religious belief but against all modes of veneration. The danger is then a danger not to Johnson but to the perception of his superiority that sustains the *Life*'s inner world. As the irony of the philosophes has been turned on Christianity, making the believer appear a mere foolish creature of superstition, it could as easily be turned on those who gather around Johnson's philosophic throne, reducing their veneration of his moral character to a weak and credulous admiration of what is not admirable.

To understand this danger fully, we must, in a manner of speaking, reverse the controlling perspective of the *Life*, gaze inward on Johnson as he might appear from the outer world of his antagonists. Now, instead of a moral hero whose powers of mind and utterance create a refuge from spiritual anxiety for those around him, we have a narrow-minded dogmatizer surrounded by foolish admirers, the Johnson described in Horace Walpole's *Memoirs of the Reign of George III*: "Johnson was an odious and mean character. . . . His manners were sordid, supercilious and brutal; his style ridiculously bombastic and vicious; and, in one word, with all the pedantry he had all the gigantic littleness of a country schoolmaster" (IV.314,*n*.3). To see Johnson in this light for even a moment is to confront the sense in which moral heroism involves a choice of moral perspective.

The perspective of Walpole is not, of course, identical with the perspective of the philosophes: it is the attitude of *nil admirari* that the moral dilettante employs in his dealings with a world in which some men, at least, hold fixed opinions and beliefs. Yet Walpole's detached superiority is at one extreme of a spectrum that reaches at the other to the powerful mockery of a Voltaire; and at one or another point on the spectrum may be located the varieties of irony or mockery or moral detachment that characterize the outer world of the *Life*. We thus encounter here the symbolic or dramatic principle that separates the outer from the inner world of the biographical story: if the *Life* simply ignored the possibility of an irony or mockery that showed its hero in a ludicrous light, no problems of perspective or moral choice would exist. It is by recognizing such a possibility, by positing an internal tension between mockery and veneration, that the *Life* draws the circumference of its inner world.

This is why, for instance, the presence of Edward Gibbon at the meetings of the Literary Club—the gathering of congenial spirits that is the very center of the inner world—is so often felt as a lurking or unsettling presence, setting off the same vague tremors as Satan's arrival in Paradise. For Gibbon is preeminently the freethinker whose weapons against the established order are irony and mockery, and who in the guise of an historian has joined the assault of the philosophes on the central doctrines of Christianity. He figures in the *Life* as a writer "noted for introducing a kind of sneering infidelity into his Historical Writings" (II.67), and his *Decline and Fall* as a work "written in a very mellifluous style, but which, under pretext of another subject, contained much artful infidelity" (II.447). He is, at other times, the "notorious infidel" at whose identity the alert reader of the *Life* is meant to guess. As an envoy of the antagonistic outer world who has improbably found his way to the heart of the Johnsonian circle, Gibbon is a constant reminder that the distinction between the two worlds is moral rather than (as it might otherwise seem) merely social.

Simply to dwell on the principle of internal tension that divides the larger world of the *Life* into two moral spheres, however, is to suggest that those two spheres exist in a kind of uneasy balance: at the center we should have Johnson surrounded by those who venerate him (and whose veneration might derive from weakness or credulity) and in the outer sphere figures whose beliefs are simply different from or opposed to Johnson's (and whose minds might be as powerful as his). To see that this is a false description of the dramatic structure of the *Life* is at once to see that the tension is resolved in dramatic rather than moral or intellectual terms. It is not that the *Life* posits the existence of its inner world from the beginning of the biographical story, but that the story, from the days of his obscurity to his final eminence, is an account of how that world comes into being.

The *Life* as a whole, I have said, posits a world in which there operates something like a moral law of gravity, a principle of attraction that draws characters of moral or intellectual substance toward the Johnsonian center. The inner world of the *Life* is formed of elements drawn out of a realm of spiritual chaos, and it emerges as a moral order precisely as these come to revolve around the central figure of Johnson. In this context it is the principle of moral order itself that sustains the inner sphere, for to remain beyond its circumference is to choose chaos over order, to choose, out of vanity, or blindness, or malevolent intent, darkness over light. The outer world of the philosophes, of skeptics like Hume and Voltaire and atheists like Holbach, is thus a world of blind egoism and ceaseless railing against an ontological order that transcends the self. To enter the inner world, where Johnson as an object of veneration represents and defends that order, is to renounce the egoism of the outer sphere.

So long as the illusion of a stable narrative and dramatic structure is sustained by a notion of Boswell's relation to an imaginary audience outside the story, we have an overwhelming dramatic movement that works against the discontinuities of the text. The sequence of deconstructions that moves us steadily toward a vacuum at the center of the *Life* began, we saw, in the antithetical relation between the idealized and disembodied Johnson whom his readers imagine to exist as a presence behind the moral writings and the rough and uncouth Johnson whom they encounter in the actual surroundings of drawing room and tavern. Yet while Boswell's relation to his audience appears as a controlling ratio, all this demands reinterpretation as an integrative movement.

As an integrative movement, one which draws toward the Johnsonian center the worthiest souls of the age, the centripetal process always begins when one encounters the idealized Johnson of the writings and is moved to seek out the living moralist. This we have seen to be Boswell's case.

Then there is Reynolds, who "had, from the first reading
of his Life of Savage, conceived a very high admiration of
Johnson's powers of writing. His conversation no less delighted him; and he cultivated his acquaintance with the
laudable zeal of one who was ambitious of general im-
provement" (I.245). There is, once again, Langton, whose
friendship with Johnson commences "soon after the conclusion of his Rambler; which that gentleman, then a youth,
had read with so much admiration, that he came to London
chiefly with the view of endeavouring to be introduced to
its authour," and whose first meeting with Johnson we
have already seen:

> From perusing his writings, he fancied he should see a
> decent, well-drest, in short, a remarkably decorous phi-
> losopher. Instead of which, down from his bed-chamber,
> about noon, came, as newly risen, a huge uncouth figure,
> with a little dark wig which scarcely covered his head,
> and his clothes hanging loose about him. But his conver-
> sation was so rich, so animated, and so forcible, and his
> religious and political notions so congenial with those in
> which Mr. Langton had been educated, that he conceived
> for him that veneration and attachment which he ever
> preserved. (I.247-48)

As we have seen, the emphasis on Johnson's conversation, on an intellectual blaze that obliterates the peculiari-
ties of his appearance and leaves the mind filled only with
an impression of overwhelming power of intellect, is
throughout the *Life* associated with a theme of the logos
that identifies ennobling and genuine eloquence with its
origin in divine intelligence. This is the context in which
the Johnson revealed in conversation represents, for inhabitants of the *Life*'s inner world, a moral center: "but all
these slovenly particularities," we recall Boswell saying
after he has described his first view of Johnson at home,
"were forgotten the moment that he began to talk" (I.396).
This is the moral hero whose conversation so casts its spell

over Boswell as narrator ("I recollect with admiration an animating blaze of eloquence, which rouzed every intellectual power in me to the highest pitch" [I.460]) and over members of his circle "that they regretted when it was interrupted, or ceased, and could exclaim in Milton's language, 'With thee conversing, I forget all time' " (IV.346). An impression of Johnson's conversation as embodying an intelligence nearly divine can be sustained only as long as the inhabitants of the *Life*'s inner world seek and discover behind it the presence of an heroic spirit expressing itself in spoken discourse. Yet as long as Boswell's relation to an imaginary and external audience brings the discontinuities of the text into one particular alignment, this is precisely what we see them doing, venerating a Johnson of their own creation and wondering only occasionally, when some anomalous utterance threatens their image of the man as magisterial conversationalist, whether their Johnson is not a construct after all. The truth of their creation, what they perceive as in a mirror, is the truth of the spiritual anxiety that moves them to venerate the Johnson they construct.

The theme of the logos thus controls the movement that draws the inhabitants of the *Life*'s inner world toward a Johnsonian center, for so far as the logos involves a notion of presence behind utterance it testifies to a desire to discover behind the visible appearance of things an invisible order that imposes meaning on an existence otherwise meaningless. For Boswell or Burke or Reynolds, discovering an invisible Johnsonian presence behind the discontinuities of Johnson's discourse corresponds in the social sphere to the discovery of a ruling intelligence behind the natural order, with language or the logos as the axis connecting human discourse with the realm of the divine. The imaginary Johnson in whose presence they move is as noble as the unrecognized metaphysical impulse that creates him.

The inner world of the *Life* begins to dissolve as a world, however, the moment we see the Johnson who occupies its center as a creation of his admirers, a fiction of presence imposed on the discontinuities of his discourse from without. Yet in the moment of dissolution we glimpse another truth not unrelated to the vision of utterance that sustains the inner world, that truth of mind as speech or discourse embodied in the conversation scenes. For language, even as it encloses a world of meaning separate from every other world, a sphere of signification denying all metaphysical notions of presence, yet means or signifies in its own terms, lies in opposing relation to mindless or meaningless randomness.

The power of this vision of language, even as it works to dissolve the illusion of an inner world in the *Life*, works on a deeper level to sustain it. For what is dissolved is only the notion of a Johnsonian presence behind Johnsonian utterance, and what remains is the mystery of utterance itself. The inhabitants of the inner world are drawn not toward the Johnson they imagine or create, but toward the mystery of discourse at the supreme level, toward a revelation of mind not expressed through but embodied in language, a center purified of presence and emptied of everything but its own meaning. And this remains true when we see that the inhabitants of the inner world are not themselves present except as discontinuous orders of discourse composing the text.

To see that the mystery of discourse or language existing on its own terms underlies the meaning of that dramatic movement that, on another level, brings the inner world of the *Life* into being is to understand how its meaning derives from the reversal of an earlier perspective. For now it is not that the anomalies in Johnson's conversation, those abrupt discontinuities that threaten to undermine or subvert all stable illusions of Johnsonian presence, must be explained away by his admirers as moments of laxity or sophistry or roughness, but that they exert their own fascination as reminders of a truth that lies behind all illusions of presence, a truth that reveals the center of mind as language or utterance.

The gravitational attraction of the Johnsonian center must at last be seen in these terms, as an attraction that exists not in spite of but because of the discontinuities of Johnsonian utterance. "At different times," we recall Boswell saying, "he seemed a different man," and what haunts Boswell as he says this is not Johnson's character as a man but "the display of argument and fancy in his talk." There is anxiety in the remark, but anxiety only on the level at which there exists the illusion of a Johnsonian presence behind speech. On a deeper level there is the steady fascination, felt by every inhabitant of the inner world of the *Life*, of a display of argument and fancy that moves the mind to a contemplation of discourse as a separate reality.

Yet it is only on the level of illusions of Johnsonian presence that we see the image of Johnson as conversationalist as the source of the gravitational power that draws the ordinary and the eminent into his orbit, that transforms an ordinary eighteenth-century social world into the inner world of the *Life*. At the center of this world, a kind of synecdoche of the whole, is the Club, and the presence of so many distinguished men around Johnson's philosophic throne is the *Life*'s guarantee of his moral and intellectual stature. A modern reader of the *Life* is likely to hurry over Boswell's listing of its membership as being merely perfunctory and drily factual. The list should, on the contrary, be read slowly and with a growing sense of awe, like the catalogue of ships in the *Iliad*:

Between the time of its formation, and the time at which this work is passing through the press (June, 1792,) the following persons, now dead, were members of it: Mr. Dunning, (afterwards Lord Ashburton,) Mr. Samuel Dyer, Mr. Garrick, Dr. Shipley Bishop of St. Asaph, Mr. Vesey, Mr. Thomas Warton and Dr. Adam Smith. The present members are, Mr. Burke, Mr. Langton, Lord Charlemont, Sir Robert Chambers, Dr. Percy Bishop of Dromore, Dr. Barnard Bishop of Killaloe, Dr. Marlay Bishop of Clonfert, Mr. Fox, Dr. George Fordyce, Sir William Scott, Sir Joseph Banks, Sir Charles Bunbury, Mr. Windham of Norfolk, Mr. Sheridan, Mr. Gibbon, Sir William Jones, Mr. Colman, Mr. Steevens, Dr. Burney, Dr. Joseph Warton, Mr. Malone, Lord Ossory, Lord Spencer, Lord Lucan, Lord Palmerston, Lord Eliot, Lord Macartney, Mr. Richard Burke, junior, Sir William Hamilton, Dr. Warren, Mr. Courtenay, Dr. Hinchcliffe Bishop of Peterborough, the Duke of Leeds, Dr. Douglas Bishop of Salisbury, and the writer of this account. (I.479)

At the same time, the Club is only the center of the *Life's* inner world, for in the course of the story that world expands to become a microcosm of English society, embracing the age from the drawing room to the gutter: "volumes would be required to contain a list of his numerous and various acquaintance. . . . He associated with persons the most widely different in manners, abilities, rank and accomplishments. He was at once the companion of the brilliant Colonel Forrester of the guards, who wrote 'The Polite Philosopher' and the aukward and uncouth Robert Levet; of Lord Thurlow, and Mr. Sastres, the Italian master; and has dined one day with the beautiful, gay, and fascinating Lady Craven, and the next with good Mrs. Gardiner, the tallow-chandler, on Snow-hill" (III.21-22). For it is not manners or abilities, rank or accomplishments, that give one entrance to the inner sphere, but the same perception of Johnson as a superior man held by its other inhabitants.

Indeed, the inner world of the *Life* is one in which social distinctions dissolve and a new order crystallizes around the figure of Johnson whenever he speaks. One recalls Langton's account of a typical evening: " 'among the gen-

tlemen were Lord Althorpe . . . Lord Macartney, Sir Joshua
Reynolds, Lord Lucan, Mr. Wraxal . . . Dr. Warren, Mr.
Pepys, the Master in Chancery . . . and Dr. Barnard, the
Provost of Eton. As soon as Dr. Johnson was come in and
had taken a chair, the company began to collect round
him, till they became not less than four, if not five, deep;
those behind standing, and listening over the heads of those
that were sitting near him' " (III.425-26). In all the great
conversation scenes of the *Life* a similar dynamic is at work,
giving us the single timeless center of a world that Johnson
rules through the power of his mind and utterance—or, as
Paul Alkon puts it in a brilliant essay on the *Life*, a "sustained association of Johnson with that English milieu
which is made to define the value of his life and which in
turn *creates* throughout Boswell's narrative a sense of that
life as a single action."[4]

The emblem of all such scenes, I have said, is Johnson's
meeting with George III, which in symbolic or dramatic
terms is the meeting of one sovereign with another. The
episode is too familiar to demand detailed discussion, but
it must be remembered that it too takes its place among
the conversation scenes: " 'I found his Majesty wished I
should talk,' " says Johnson at the beginning of his own
account of the meeting, " 'and I made it my business to
talk' " (II.42). When Johnson does begin to speak, we are,
as always in the major scenes of the *Life*, in a sovereignty
where stature is determined only by power of mind, where
Johnson reigns supreme and even his lawful monarch is
only another inhabitant of the inner circle gathered around
his philosophic throne. Johnson as biographical hero is at
such moments identical with the mythopoeic Johnson of
Courtenay's poem, ordained by nature's gifts to rule mankind, and to create by sheer force of character a sphere of
moral stability in the midst of spiritual dissolution.

[4] Paul K. Alkon, "Boswellian Time," *Studies in Burke and His Time*
(Spring 1973), 239-56.

Yet all this derives from an illusion of narrative stability imposed on the *Life* by a notion of Boswell's relation to an imaginary audience external to the story, that controlling antithetical ratio which brings into alignment the discontinuous orders of discourse composing the text. To understand the alignment that separates the *Life* into inner and outer worlds, we must see how the illusion is created, why it is so to speak written into the text itself. For to see this is, in the end, to see how the illusion survives our awareness that Boswell is not after all a mediating presence, that his narration is only one discontinuous order of discourse among others, and that his imaginary audience is not a presence external to the story but only the implied outer limit of his narration.

The illusion of audience as a continuous and external presence does, remarkably enough, survive our awareness of the discontinuous nature of the text of the *Life*, and when we see why this is so we come to see simultaneously why it remains possible to discuss the *Life* as a stable narrative structure. For what I am calling the illusion of stability is something created by the purely formal nature of the relation between narrator and audience in any narrative structure, the subject-object or I-Thou relation that is an underlying condition of all modes of discourse. What is not illusion, what emerges within the formal context as a new principle of antithetical ratio controlling and finally enclosing the discontinuities of the text, is the dynamics of Boswell's relation to the audience he imagines.

The illusion of an inner and outer world in the *Life* begins, I said, in the moment we recognize Boswell as the only voice in the *Life* who addresses an audience he imagines to exist external to the biographical story—this is why we see him, in conventional terms, as the narrator of the story, why he appears as a consciousness mediating between the audience of the *Life* and all that occurs within its world. The notion of Johnson as the moral center of an inner sphere, of an invisible law of moral gravitation that draws toward the Johnsonian center the worthiest souls of the age, of an outer sphere of egoism and empty mockery, thus derives in its totality from a notion of controlling antithesis denied by the text. How, then, does it come to survive in other terms?

The answer lies in a movement that ultimately posits the relation of the *Life* as a whole to a center of moral judgment external to itself, in the emergence of audience as a timeless presence in relation to a world existing outside of time. For it is not simply that the division of the *Life* into an inner and outer world is on one level controlled by Boswell's relation to an imaginary audience, though this remains the illusion that dissolves under the antithetical pressures of the text. It is that in the last instance the same division, now assumed as a moral reality, comes to control Boswell's relation to the audience he addresses, recreating on a higher level the grand antithesis that brackets or encloses the discontinuities of the text.

At the final level of analysis, that is, the structure of the *Life* demands that we come to terms with something like the phenomenological principle of intentionality. So long as Boswell's narration simply implies the existence of an inner and outer world within the biographical story, the alignment of elements that gives us that world is arbitrary and illusive, something that cannot survive our discovery of Boswell as a solitary voice within the text. In the moment when Boswell's narration posits an audience which, on just the same terms as the inhabitants of the biographical story, must choose to enter or remain forever outside the inner world of the *Life*, the text as a whole posits a center of moral judgment external to itself.

The narrative stability of the *Life* finally comes to rest on this principle of an implied relation to an external center of moral judgment, something that, unlike the illusion of center and presence also written into the text, is never denied by its discontinuities. Herein lies its similarity as a text to the principle of intentionality in action:

when Luther threw an inkwell at the devil, phenomenology tells us, the meaning of his action, considered purely and abstractly as an action, did not derive from the existence or nonexistence of evil spirits; the devil is, so to speak, written into the intentionality of the action, is that object without which it becomes meaningless or incomprehensible as an action. A similar principle controls the final relation between the *Life* and its imaginary audience.

Within this context it becomes meaningless to assert that it is merely an illusion that the world of the *Life* is divided into an inner and outer sphere, and that the dramatic principle controlling the division is a tension between ironic mockery and sincere veneration. For what is crucial now is that from the opening pages of the *Life* Boswell as it were looks straight in the eye of an imagined reader who is wholly, even painfully, aware of the existence of its two worlds, and who is assumed to feel the tension between them as a moral pressure on his own response to Johnson. From a sphere somewhere outside the action of the work, this imagined reader is thus offered the same choice as those within it: to enter the inner world of the *Life* and perceive Johnson as a superior being, or to resist the gravitational attraction of the Johnsonian center and remain, superior and aloof, in the outer sphere of those who mock such veneration.

At the same time, the overwhelming centripetal movement that draws the inhabitants of the *Life*'s inner world into the Johnsonian sphere is assumed to have a similar effect on its imagined reader, and the dramatic thrust of the story is toward the inclusion rather than the exclusion of its audience. It is not simply that an invitation to join a circle that includes such men as Reynolds and Burke—to see Johnson as they see him—sets up a powerful gravitational attraction, but that (as Boswell shows himself to be constantly aware) the imagined reader is exposed to Johnson in just the same way as those who inhabit the inner world. The conversation scenes of the *Life* are a present reality lived as much by the reader as by those who figure in them, and he or she is in this sense an actual participant in the intellectual drama. And no one present when Johnson speaks, no matter how resistant to the idea of veneration, can escape the awesomeness of his personal presence:

> Before Johnson came we talked a good deal of him; Ramsey said he had always found him a very polite man, and that he treated him with great respect, which he did very sincerely. I said I worshipped him. ROBERTSON. 'But some of you spoil him; you should not worship him; you should worship no man.' BOSWELL. 'I cannot help worshipping him, he is so much superiour to other men.' ROBERTSON. 'In criticism, and in wit in conversation, he is no doubt very excellent; but in other respects he is not above other men. . . .' BOSWELL. 'His power of reasoning is very strong, and he has a peculiar art of drawing characters, which is as rare as good portrait painting.' SIR JOSHUA REYNOLDS. 'He is undoubtedly admirable in this; but, in order to mark the characters which he draws, he overcharges them, and gives people more than they really have, whether of good or bad.'
>
> No sooner did he, of whom we had been thus talking so easily, arrive, than we were all as quiet as a school upon the entrance of the head-master. . . . (III.331-32)

The issue, once again, is perspective as moral choice, and it is almost possible to reconstruct the drama of choice (for the imagined reader) from such a scene as this. At the center of the circle of veneration stands Boswell, whose need of the spiritual reassurance he discovers in Johnson's presence is so great as to make him a *naif*, an admirer of Johnson so uncritical as to become an easy object of mockery. On one side stand all those who, like Robertson, are simply unable to see Johnson as a superior being: from the rattling Mr. Edwards to sneering dilettantes like Walpole to such outright antagonists as Hume or Gibbon, these are the inhabitants of the outer sphere. On the other side stand those who, like Sir Joshua, perceive Johnson as a superior man even as they remain aware of his weaknesses—for whom, indeed, his failings are inseparable from his greatness—and whose perspective is ultimately the perspective of the inner world.

What finally resolves the unreal tension between pure mockery and pure veneration is the *Life*'s steady undermining of the notion that admiration of Johnson, to be sincere, must be uncritical. This is why Boswell, for instance, once established in his role as uncritical admirer of his hero, nonetheless establishes a steady counterpoint of dissent in matters of opinion: "I expressed a liking for Mr. Francis Osborne's works, and asked him what he thought of that writer. He answered, 'A conceited·fellow. Were a man to write so now, the boys would throw stones at him.' He however did not alter my opinion of a favourite authour . . ." (II.193). Or of Swift, or of Fielding, or of Gray, or of a hundred matters of social or political belief— for example, the war against the American colonies—where the opinions of the narrator oppose those of his hero.[5] Even in Boswell's case (and the imagined reader is to see Boswell's perspective as extreme) veneration means something other than uncritical adulation.

Along with Johnson's occasional eccentricities of opinion go his personal eccentricities and the roughness of manner so often mentioned in the *Life*, weaknesses that once again demand to be seen as inseparable from his brilliance as a conversationalist. For a willingness to talk for victory, to argue with overpowering wit and energy and resourcefulness against every opponent, will necessarily result in a large number of social casualties. Yet the imagined audience of the *Life* is assumed to respond to this roughness as do inhabitants of the *Life*'s inner world, even to the point of understanding that Johnson himself may become a casualty:

[5] See Paul K. Alkon, "Boswell's Control of Aesthetic Distance," *University of Toronto Quarterly* (January 1969), 174-91.

I was at this time myself a water-drinker, upon trial, by Johnson's recommendation. JOHNSON. 'Boswell is a bolder combatant than Sir Joshua: he argues for wine without the help of wine; but Sir Joshua with it.' SIR JOSHUA REYNOLDS. 'But to please one's company is a strong motive.' JOHNSON. (who, from drinking only water, supposed every body who drank wine to be elevated,) 'I won't argue any more with you, Sir. You are too far gone.' SIR JOSHUA. 'I should have thought so indeed, Sir, had I made such a speech as you have now done.' JOHNSON. (drawing himself in, and, I really thought blushing,) 'Nay, don't be angry. I did not mean to offend you.' (III.328-29)

As the imagined audience of the *Life* is drawn more and more into its inner world, is assumed by Boswell to have succumbed to the inevitable attraction of the Johnsonian center, a countermovement of exclusion begins. For while Boswell continues to gaze directly at his imagined reader, there are now frequent side-glances at a class of readers who remain impervious to Johnson's greatness. Most often, Boswell's acknowledgment that such readers exist takes the form of a defense of his biographical method: "I cannot allow any fragment whatever that floats in my memory concerning the great subject of this work to be lost. Though a small particular may appear trifling to some, it will be relished by others; while every little spark adds something to the general blaze: and to please the true, candid, warm admirers of Johnson, and in any degree increase the splendour of his reputation, I bid defiance to the shafts of ridicule, or even of malignity" (III.190).

Yet biographical method is only an excuse for emphasizing the *Life*'s division of its audience, as it has already divided those within its world, into two spheres. The imagined reader whom Boswell addresses throughout is now assumed to be among the company of "true, candid, warm admirers of Johnson" (the language is identical with that Boswell uses to describe the attitude of such members of the inner circle as Reynolds and Langton), and to share his own perception of those who have willfully chosen to remain in the outer sphere, ready to hurl shafts of ridicule (Walpole, Gibbon, etc.) or even of malignity (Hume, Voltaire, etc.). On this choice the *Life* in effect makes a severe moral judgment. It is the judgment of Guyon and the Palmer on Grill, who chooses to retain his Circean form even after the Bower of Bliss has been destroyed and Acrasia's other victims have become human again:

> Said Guyon, "See the mind of beastly man,
> That hath so soone forgot the excellence
> Of his creation, when he life began,
> That now he chooseth, with vile difference,
> To be a beast, and lacke intelligence."
> To whom the Palmer thus, "The donghill kind
> Delights in filth and foule incontinence:
> Let Grill be Grill, and have his hoggish mind,
> But let us hence depart, whilest wether serves and wind."

By the end of the biographical story, excluded by the *Life*'s own dramatic principles, this nonaudience of antagonistic readers is simply assumed to have disappeared—or, more properly, to have fallen by the wayside, victim of its own egoism or insensibility. For the great movement that begins with Boswell's early withdrawal from the scene ("I now relieve the readers of this Work from any further personal notice of its authour" [IV.380]) and ends with Johnson's death suspends Boswell's relation to his imagined audience. What remains, in the *Life*'s public and elegiac account of Johnson's passing, is an objectification and enlargement of Boswell's own perception of his hero, a demonstration that the perspective of the inner sphere is the perspective of an age. It is an anonymous spokesman for the age who delivers the final verdict: " 'He has made a chasm, which not only nothing can fill up, but which nothing has a tendency to fill up.—Johnson is dead.—Let us go to the next best:—there is nobody;—no man can be said to put you in mind of Johnson' " (IV.420-21).

At this moment the imagined audience of the *Life*, whose view of Johnson has until now only been assumed in some vague and necessary sense to be retrospective, is located in a timeless reality. For the *Life* itself, as Boswell once says of his earlier *Tour to the Hebrides*, is imagined as sailing "unhurt along the stream of time," and the drama of moral choice in which its biographical hero emerges as a genuinely great man is one that must be repeated whenever its first leaf is turned and the story begins again. It is the timeless perspective of its imagined audience that ultimately allows the *Life* to portray Johnson as a figure outside of time: "such was SAMUEL JOHNSON, a man whose talents, acquirements, and virtues, were so extraordinary, that the more his character is considered, the more he will be regarded by the present age, and by posterity, with admiration and reverence."

EPILOGUE

So FAR as the argument of this study represents not merely an elucidation of the structure of the *Life of Johnson* but a pondering of the meaning of discontinuity in narrative, it suggests that the assumptions of the objective and deconstructionist theories of interpretation are not irreconcilable after all. For what the *Life* tells us about literary structure must be true at a general level whenever we encounter the problem of narrative discontinuity, and this in itself suggests the possibility of working out a complete grammar of discontinuity in literature. That work must be left to other hands than mine; I will be content if I have contributed to the enterprise.

The question that remains, and that occurs to me with some urgency as I pause to reflect on the broader implications of my own argument, is why formal or objective theory and the newer theory of deconstruction are so widely perceived to be locked in a fatal conflict. Part of the explanation, I suspect, is that Derrida, the guiding light of the deconstructionist program, has chosen to picture deconstruction as involving a gigantic clash of metaphysical systems. This has its value, a very considerable value, because Derrida is not a literary critic but a philosopher, but it muddies the waters when we are trying to think clearly about deconstruction in literary interpretation. The greater mystery is why the vocabulary of conflict or crisis is today employed so universally by critical theorists themselves, whose business it is to think coolly and rigorously through the claims of competing theories. On the deconstructionist side of the debate, however, the vocabulary of crisis is understandable enough: Geoffrey Hartman writing about literary criticism and its discontents, Hillis Miller obliquely pursuing a twisting path through Indo-European etymologies in response to a perfectly straightforward critique of deconstructionist theory by M. H. Abrams, are writers enacting the theoretical assumptions they avow. In pure form, this is something that deconstructionist theory, at its furthest reach of Nietzschean implication, demands of its practitioners.

There is not, surely, an invitation to conflict or a portent of crisis in any of this. Quite aside from the question of whether intellectual discourse must always enact its assumptions—and it is one point of the deconstructionists that the lucidity and straightforwardness of Anglo-American criticism enact a comfortable norm of intellectual complacency, an avoidance of deeper issues—such enactment is an old and honorable tradition in western thought. Behind it stands nothing less than the massive authority of Plato's dialogues, the dialogue form itself enacting a drama of rational critique—probabilistic truth and critical analysis *in action*—and the same strain is traceable at least through the self-denying propositions of Wittgenstein's *Tractatus*.

On the other side of the debate, however, along with Abrams's calm and reasoned argument, we encounter a new strain of resistance to deconstructionist theory. Though examples of the sort of resistance I have in mind now appear almost monthly in the learned journals,[1] an early and noteworthy example is Gerald Graff's essay, published in 1977 in *The American Scholar*, on what he elects to call fear and trembling at Yale. The essay is noteworthy not because it directly attacks deconstruction (it is also about Harold Bloom and other nondeconstructionists) or because it contains anything of theoretical import. Its noteworthiness lies solely in its tone.

In writing purely in a derisory vein, and moreover, with no grasp of the theoretical ideas that the deconstructionists are attempting to inject into the mainstream of critical

[1] And, increasingly, in the popular press. See Peter Shaw, "Degenerate Criticism: The Dismal State of English Studies," *Harper's* (October 1979), pp. 93-99.

thinking, hostile writers seem to me to run the risk of precipitating a genuine crisis, a moral crisis almost, in literary studies. For such writers put themselves in much the same relation to deconstructionist interpretation as, in Froude's wonderful description, the established order found itself in relation to Carlyle's newly published *Past and Present*: "the representatives of the Religiones Licitae, the conventional varieties of permitted practice and speculation, found themselves encountered by a novel element which would assimilate with none of them, which disturbed all their digestions, yet which they equally could not ignore."[2]

There is, in the response of Graff and other such writers to the emergent body of deconstructionist and other theory, the sense of a threatened pastoral vision, the imminent disappearance of a golden age when interpretation brought to light truths about literature whose power to elucidate was simply and comfortably self-evident. We used to think of professors of literature, says Graff at the beginning of his essay, as people reasonably well paid for reading books and writing about them, "going abroad with some frequency on summer vacations, sabbaticals, and research grants, drinking Chivas Regal and Jack Daniels at parties or at professional conferences." It is not least this pastoral existence that is threatened by a degeneration of criticism into "formula, bathos, and unearned generalization."[3]

There is, I say, the threat of genuine crisis in all this, and it does not lie with the deconstructionist critics and their talk of criticism in crisis or criticism *as* crisis—that, once again, is the justifiable enactment of their theoretical assumptions. Nor does it lie in any direct sense with writers like Graff, insofar as they are writing merely out of an uncomfortable sense of intellectual dyspepsia, attempting to master through derision or mockery a body of ideas they

[2] *Froude's Life of Carlyle*, ed. and abr. John Clubbe (Columbus: Ohio State University Press), p. 417.

[3] Gerald Graff, "Fear and Trembling at Yale," *The American Scholar* (Autumn 1977), 467, 478.

have not attempted to understand. The threat of crisis lies rather among those, perhaps the vast majority in literary studies, who pursue their work on ground lower than the airy regions where theoretical debate is conducted.

There are many spokesmen for the inhabitants of this lower ground, and their number is swelling so rapidly that denunciation of the present state of literary studies threatens soon to become the major enterprise within literary studies. Yet one such denunciation by William D. Schaefer stands out, at least to my mind, among the rest.[4] For the most part, Schaefer's observations echo the usual complaints of those who see literary studies in crisis: English departments have not packaged their product attractively enough, too much emphasis is placed on publication, and so on. Yet we encounter something else, a tone of pure and outraged bafflement: we in literary studies have joined our colleagues the scientists and social scientists

> in developing a language and a manner of presentation to ensure that the layman could not understand what we were talking about, guarding the holy grail by deconstructing ever more elaborate machinery around it, creating exotic vocabularies and no end of deep structures to prevent the uninitiated from tampering with the sacred mysteries. We have now, I believe, nearly perfected the art of unintelligibility to the extent that in many cases we no longer understand ourselves.[5]

It is not simply that literary interpretation is now sometimes written in impenetrable language, but that so much literary interpretation, when it does manage to make itself understood, is so patently vacuous, circular, or intellectually maladroit. Schaefer lists as evidence extracts from readers' reports on articles rejected for publication in *PMLA*:

[4] William D. Schaefer, "Still Crazy After All These Years," *ADE Bulletin*, 55 (November 1977), 1-8.
[5] Schaefer, "Still Crazy," 4.

what they tell me is that we are playing games with literature and with scholarship. They are not happy games, nor are they harmless; careers depend on them as we force ourselves through ever more frenzied attempts to discover new things to say or, more often, new ways to say old things. To recognize that no one really reads most of this junk is to miss the point. It is a matter of wasted time, of misdirected energies.[6]

If there is a genuine crisis in literary studies now, surely we discover it in the tenor of these remarks. For Schaefer may be taken as representative of the widespread dismay provoked by current theoretical speculation. This is how literary studies look from the valley as one peers upward at the mountaintop, obscured in mist and cloud, where invisible theorists hurl bolts of lightning at one another. Literary interpretation has become trivialized, has degenerated into empty ingenuity, has become mindlessly self-indulgent. Literary studies have, in a word, ceased to matter.

Yet there is more, much more, to the crisis than this, I believe. For if literary studies were pursued in a vacuum, or by the sort of wealthy amateurs who, in the eighteenth century and later, contributed so much to the later pursuit of professional scholarship, there would be little ground for dismay. The crisis occurs because, unlike the eighteenth-century amateur or those earlier glorious amateurs the Renaissance humanists, we who profess literary studies now do so in what Geoffrey Hartman has called "a grimmer, more realistic" setting:

We teach and write in a mass culture. Though Erasmus and Comenius did not neglect elementary education, teachers of literature in a mass culture are obliged to become *primarily* grammarians, spelling masters, and instructors of civics. Even the revival of rhetoric as an

6 Schaefer, "Still Crazy," 3.

instrument of literary analysis—the poet Hopkins called rhetoric the *teachable* part of literature—is understandable in this light.[7]

The real crisis in literary studies has little to do with the self-indulgence or empty ingenuity of modern interpretation. It is, for anxious commentators like Schaefer, the profound and growing tension between interpretation and its modern setting in the university, the sense of anomaly that comes when one observes a relatively small group of professional scholars writing exclusively for one another, pursuing their studies in the midst of a society rapidly declining into actual illiteracy. This is the climate in which interpretation appears from the outside as a self-indulgent game played on by mere egoists in a dark scene of ruin and chaos, and in which theorists, with their abstruse concerns, seem the most self-indulgent of all.

These thoughts were often in my mind as I wrote *Language and Logos*, along with the question of whether they were to be mentioned even in an epilogue to my main argument. For in literary studies whatever is merely topical or temporary wears badly, and the current fashion of attempting to "justify" literary studies or humanistic study itself has always struck me as a queasy business, an exercise in what Carlyle, in the large and special meaning he gave to the word, called insincerity. Yet on reflection I see, or think I see, that these are not matters topical or temporary; they belong to a long and valuable tradition of thinking about the nature of language itself.

This is not to say that the current mood of crisis does not possess its transitory aspect. When commentators respond in the manner we have seen to deconstructionist theory, for instance, and when we recognize in their mockery a summons to defend a pastoral vision of afternoon sherries and obvious truths, it is evident that there has

[7] Hartman, "Literary Criticism and Its Discontents," *Critical Inquiry*, 3 (Winter 1976), 206.

been some failure of historical sense. For the pastoral period they remember was really the relatively short time, no more than fifteen or twenty years, during which the lessons of the formal or objective theory were being assimilated by literary interpretation generally. On the other side of this pastoral interlude were critical wars quite as clamorous as those of the present day.

The grand moral of our current conflicts in theory and interpretation may be drawn, I think, even while we are still surrounded by a confusion of noise and dust, from that earlier period of controversy, the period when a group of theorists and critics, René Wellek, W. K. Wimsatt, Monroe Beardsley, Cleanth Brooks, and others, achieved their own critical mass at Yale and exerted a profound influence on literary studies. The vision of literary autonomy urged in their writings, of literature as a permanent and timeless order of meaning, is now familiar to all who pursue literary studies. It was anything but clear at the time, when the "new" criticism, with its talk of irony and paradox and ambiguity, was also frequently accused of excessive ingenuities.

The outlines of a similar situation may be glimpsed now, and the lesson to be drawn is that what appears from the outside as crisis appears within as a time of extraordinary creative ferment. If there is cause for dismay, it is that a generation of scholars, older and younger as well, may awaken to find themselves operating in an intellectual world grown suddenly alien; there are few sadder moments for a teacher, said Einstein, than when he discovers that the language and methods and problems of his students are no longer his own. Yet should this occur, as it did for a generation of genetic or biographical critics when the "new" criticism won its victories, it is inseparable from the nature of the enterprise.

Another transitory aspect of the current sense of crisis derives, it seems to me, from a certain naiveté about the nature of theory and interpretation—indeed, of theory and explanation in any area of inquiry whatever. The charges of self-indulgence and excessive ingenuity in literary studies now imply, surely, that there is a fixed body of meaning in literature which it is the business of interpretation to liberate, and that when interpretation goes beyond this it is in some demonstrable way battening upon itself. In simple terms, this is the sort of resistance one expects to encounter in the classroom: interpretation is at fault, finally, for making literature more complex than it really is.

Such questions cannot be answered either simply or shortly, for the only really convincing answer would be an entire epistemology of inquiry along the lines of that which philosophers are attempting to work out in the limited area of the empirical sciences (I have in mind the work of Popper, Polanyi, and others). Yet what always comes to light in such studies of theory, conjecture, hypothesis, and explanation is surely of the utmost importance for literary studies; the finding is that theory and explanation (interpretation), while they in one sense discover the truth about some sphere of reality, also create the sphere of reality about which they discover new truths.

The world of mathematics is thus unimaginably more complex today than it was two centuries or even a century ago, and this is because new mathematical theories have created a more complex world. In physics, which illustrates the point most dramatically because it seems at one level to be about a "real" or "physical" world, the story is one with which all educated people are today familiar: the movement from a world where the sun rose over a flat earth to the orderly universe of Newtonian or classical mechanics, with suns and planets gravely circling one another in a rational minuet, to the ceaseless dance of matter and energy pictured by quantum physics is, we say now, a story of successive paradigms and scientific revolutions.

Yet to speak of revolutions in scientific theory is to obscure the sense in which physics actually created, through theory alone, the worlds it explained. The generation that awoke to discover that the earth was a planet moving according to strict Newtonian laws around the sun did not inhabit a physical universe different from that inhabited by its ancestors; it inhabited, rather, a new and more complex universe of theory and explanation. Nor, perhaps, is such awakening possible except through a crisis at the level of abstract theory, as Einstein's resolute refusal to believe the truth of—to believe in the world created by—quantum theory bears notorious witness.

This is the context in which, if literature now appears a more complex sphere of reality than in the days before modern interpretation, it does so because interpretation has simultaneously discovered and created a universe of meaning or significance that did not exist before. To argue that the *Life of Johnson* is not merely an aging literary monument—or, as sometimes used to be said with amiable intention, a bedside book—that it is a work embodying a complex dynamic of norms and values, of problems about language and reality, is to argue only that interpretation may reveal it to embody a world previously unsuspected to exist. There is, in this, no hint of crisis.

So the mood of crisis derives in the end not from the fact that the *Life of Johnson* contains discontinuities so radical as to threaten received notions of literary structure, but from the fact that any attempt to work out a conceptual model and interpretive vocabulary adequate to the *Life* will be, as this has been, carried forward in the midst of a mass culture, a society declining into illiteracy and its universities into semiliteracy. The world of Erasmus and Comenius, the idea of human culture sustained by the literature and learning of the past, seems to be fading into ghostly insubstantiality, and the significance of literary studies in the grim landscape of the present is not yet clear. This, perhaps, is the crisis.

Yet there is more to the sense of crisis than this, I think, for in the background behind such contemporary pronouncements as William Schaefer's remarks may be glimpsed an older, deeper anxiety about literary study itself. Literary study in its most elementary and innocent modality is nothing other than reading, and for two centuries now there has been a growing fear that reading itself, or at least the reading of what we are accustomed to call literature, represents a pastoral activity merely, an abdication of the responsibilities of the world. Thus the striking contemporaneity of a passage in the *Journal* of Mark Rutherford (William Hale White) published exactly at the turn of the twentieth century:

> In these latter days of anarchy and tumult, when there is no gospel of faith and morals, when democracy seems bent on falsifying every prediction of earlier democratic enthusiasts by developing worse dangers to liberty than any which our forefathers had to encounter, and when the misery of the cities is so great, it appears absurd, not to say wrong, that we should sit still and read books. I am ashamed when I go into my own little room and open Milton or Shakespeare after looking at a newspaper or walking through the streets of London.[8]

The contemporary crisis in literary studies is not, from this point of view, so very contemporary after all. It is the latest episode in a poor drama of diminishing confidence and increasing anxiety among literate souls. This is precisely why, it seems to me, the crisis is not a genuine crisis at all—or why, rather, it is the very opposite of a crisis, a movement carrying us away from all despairing visions (a hag-ridden vision, Carlyle would have called it, a nightmare vision) and toward a new humanism, a modern version of that humanism which inspired the Renaissance of Erasmus and Colet and More. The role of deconstructionist and other new theories has been, I think, to hasten this movement toward its conclusion.

[8] Quoted in William Haley, "Will There Always Be an England," *The American Scholar* (Summer 1978), 315.

To see why this should be so, we need to think about Renaissance humanism in a new way, go beyond the usual view of the Renaissance as an episode in which classical learning and classical literature—ultimately, an ethical vision of humanity deriving not from any system of pre-ordained ontological assumptions but from a contemplation of the conditions of humanity—was recovered by the western mind. This is not to argue that the usual view is in any way mistaken. The classical perspective that emerged in the Renaissance to balance the Christian perspective of the preceding centuries was, in its historical context, the revolutionary element in the ethical and intellectual synthesis we identify now as humanism.

This is the humanism which was to assert, in Walter Jackson Bate's phrase, that man's moral and intellectual natures were identical, a movement that was to exert an uninterrupted influence in England and, to a somewhat lesser extent, on the Continent, until the waning years of the eighteenth century. Yet what underlay the movement, it seems to me, was the discovery, through the encounter with classical Latin, of language itself—not *a* language, or another language, but something essential about the nature of language that only recently has appeared in modern terms.

In a time of extraordinary linguistic consciousness—the only pure form of *self*-consciousness, perhaps—we yet need to be reminded that in most circumstances, in most ages and cultures, language is a medium as utterly transparent as the air men breathe. In this context, any moment in the history of the mind at which language is suddenly seen as opaque, as a system of meaning or signification demanding study on its own terms, is potentially revolutionary. From this discovery, within the last hundred or so years, derives linguistics in its modern form, and the same discovery marks the chasm separating modern analytic philosophy from the great speculative systems of the past.

This is to oversimplify things very greatly, I realize, but

the oversimplification bears with it an essential point: the humanism of the Renaissance to a very great extent derived from the *otherness* of classical Latin as a language, a system of signification demanding study in systematic terms (this is where the concern of the humanists with elementary education, with textbooks and grammatical classification, assumes its natural place). Without an unbroken tradition of medieval Latinity, as R. W. Southern and others have shown, the moment of discovery would have been impossible; yet it was the transparency of both medieval Latin and the vernacular languages that allowed the classical idiom to reveal language, by comparison, as opaque.

The same was true, for the humanists, of classical Greek, which, like the Latin of Virgil and Cicero, could appear as a system of meaning finished and complete, standing out in the flow of contemporary vernacular idioms as a recoverable world of significations to be mastered only as the terms of mastery in an ordinary world of linguistic transparency were set aside. It is not, I think, an act of retrospective imposition to see the humanists studying their Latin and Greek in much the same spirit as the ordinary-language philosopher today studies language in search of its hidden puzzles and confusions, or as the linguist studies language for clues to its essential nature.

To see this as humanistic in the most fundamental sense is, too, to move beyond the usual view of the Renaissance as merely an intellectual and ethical episode, no matter how revolutionary its implications when viewed in that light alone. For to understand the study of language in this deeper sense is to recover a vision only inadequately expressed in the doctrine of the logos, the teaching that language, in separating humanity from the world of trees and stones and the brute creation, reveals the human mind in its divine and eternal aspect, summons man home to the abode of God and the angelic orders.

When the notions of a divine Creator and an angelic hierarchy had faded into the realm of the mythological, this was yet a vision of language retaining a good deal of its earlier authority. For Max Müller and Archbishop Trench, arguing in the embattled nineteenth century that language represented a divinity in man that no accumulated body of Darwinian evidence could explain away, the important thing about language was still that it separated man from the brute creation and the world of trees and stones. This is the context in which the "new" or comparative philology, born in England and perfected in Germany, could enact the study of language as the human mind studying itself.

Even in modern linguistics, philosophy, and literary interpretation, the vision retains its force. For the fact remains that we are born not into a world of things or objects but into a world of language, and that a consciousness of the otherness or strangeness of language is what permits that self-consciousness—the human mind conscious of itself, through a contemplation of language, in its permanent and universal aspect—which makes our studies possible. The modern humanist is one for whom, as others swim through a world of linguistic transparency and mistake it for a world of objects, language is the primary object of thought and study and explanation.

Viewed in this light, the critical controversies of the moment may be seen to be superficial—that is, to be occurring at or near the surface of theoretical debate, where objective interpretation in the Anglo-American mode is compelled to encounter deconstruction, which, along with its opposing theoretical claims, betrays so strong a European influence. I use the word superficial now in a purely neutral and etymological sense, not to suggest that the debate is anything less than crucial—it is crucial, for only through debate can claims be sorted out and new assumptions assimilated. Nor do I want to suggest that theoretical thinking on either side has lacked either weight or seriousness; I wish to point to a similarity, if not identity, of aims at a deeper level.

Even to speak of aims, perhaps, rather than of theoretical claims or assumptions, is to gaze through to this deeper level of agreement. For objective interpretation and the objective theory of interpretation, at least, have always been humanistic in the sense I have in mind, the theory of literary autonomy being among other things an assertion that language, in its otherness or strangeness, its mysterious opacity, is the true object of humanistic study. Objective theory won its victories on narrow and conservative ground (roughly speaking, by confining itself to a privileged canon of works designated as "literary"), but it was a revived humanism that inspired its resolution to rescue literary studies from a misguided genetic or historical criticism, and provoked its attempts, through discussion of irony and paradox and ambiguity, to reveal meanings belonging to language viewed solely as language.

To view deconstructionist interpretation in relation to its own theoretical assumptions is, it seems to me, to glimpse just the same humanistic impulse in operation. Now, of course, it is not a privileged canon of works but *écriture* itself, language or discourse as a total sphere of signification, that commands the attention, but always there stands behind the enterprise the Saussurean model of language as a negative system of differences, an insistence once again on the otherness or strangeness or opacity of language. If the deconstructionist insists on this vision in more radical terms than the formal or objective theorist, it is perhaps because his vision is in the end more radically humanistic in its implications. Yet it is not, for all that, an alien vision.

At the same time, I suspect that deconstructionist theory now appears more radical in its assumptions largely because it is newer than the objective theory we have so thoroughly assimilated, and that it will appear less so as it, too, enters into the process of assimilation. We need to remind ourselves, once again, how very radical works like *The Theory of Literature* and *The Verbal Icon* appeared thirty years ago, how bitter was the controversy over such matters as intentionalism and affectivism. The issue of which theory will prove to have been more radical in its time is in any event tangential at best; what remains central is the sense in which both represent versions of a revived or modern humanism, a humanism adequate to an age altogether bleaker and more terrifying than the age of Erasmus and More.

Yet how should a new humanism, or any humanism, prove adequate to the modern age? It is this, the question of adequacy, that seems to me to underlie the present mood of crisis in literary studies—or rather, the underlying problem is a sense of total inadequacy among those who pursue such studies. This again is partly the story of an intellectual and moral anxiety going back to the early years of the nineteenth century ("I am ashamed when I go into my own little room and open Milton or Shakespeare after looking at a newspaper"), but increasingly it consists as well of a desperate confusion about the very notion of adequacy, a terror and spiritual paralysis at the heart of humane studies.

Let us conjure up, one last time, that grim specter that haunts the growing chorus of commentators who share the current sense of a crisis in the humanities. On the one hand there is a society entering into a state of actual illiteracy, universities declining into semiliteracy and worse, a world in disarray and increasingly subject to powerful forces of social disintegration. On the other hand there is a relatively small circle of literary scholars, able yet to discover a refuge within the walls of the academy, who think and write for the benefit of no one but themselves, who speak in abstruse terms only to others in the circle, who persist, in short, in going to their own little rooms and opening their Milton or Shakespeare despite the clamor beyond the windows. And among these, speaking in terms more abstruse than the rest, are those who devote themselves to theory.

This is the situation in its grimmest aspect, and against its bleak background an essential distinction stands out clearly: a sense of crisis is justified in such circumstances only if one does not glimpse in the critical controversies of the moment a modern humanism putting down its roots, a humanism working through to a vision of language and mind that promises to establish on renewed terms an almost vanished reality of cultural continuity stretching back through the Renaissance to ancient Rome and Greece. The crisis in literary studies would exist only if, at the center of controversy, there were not genuine thought or intelligence but only sham and meaningless clamor.

When it is possible to catch sight of an emergent humanism at the center of controversy, on the other hand, the notion of a small group of humanists speaking increasingly to each other is scarcely dismaying. The crisis, in such circumstances, would occur only if their numbers dwindled to nothing, if in the midst of a general decline into illiteracy there were no guardians of literacy and its values, if in a world increasingly alienated from its own intelligence there were no possessors of a humanistic vision. That literary study, and especially literary theory, speaks more and more to itself is not a comment on literary studies; it is the bleakest of comments on the age.

A humanism adequate to the age is, in this context, a humanism successfully struggling to survive in a time hostile to its values—it is adequate by very reason of its survival, and need look no further for justification. To argue otherwise, to urge that the humanities in general and literary studies in particular become adequate only as they enter into the disarray and disintegration of a mass culture painfully discovering that it has never been a culture in any genuine sense, that literacy becomes adequate only insofar as it participates in illiteracy, seems to me at best a counsel of bad faith, at worst a counsel of despair.

In speaking thus about literacy, I am aware, I invest the word with more meaning than its most common usage now accommodates. Yet it is not the mere mechanical ability to construe written or printed letters on a page that constitutes literacy, surely, but a vision of the world *in* language that, in all ages and cultures, has remained implicitly hieratic. To the literate, V. S. Naipaul somewhere remarks, the loss of literacy would seem as the loss of a sense; to the intelligent illiterate literacy appears as an encumbrance merely, the business of scribes. There, I think, we have the present sense of crisis viewed from diametrically opposing points of view: literary studies seen from within as a guardianship of the world in language, from without as the increasingly abstruse business of scribes.

So long as there is a world in language to be guarded, it seems to me, its guardianship is wholly honorable, and perhaps the more honorable as the honor appears less and less. The remarkable occurrence is that within the present closed and isolated circle of humanistic study there is emerging a new vision of the world in language, that structuralism and phenomenology and analytic philosophy and linguistics and literary theory have at last begun, each of them, to feel the strong and simultaneous influence of the others, that all signs point unwaveringly toward the emergence of a humanism as momentous in its implications as that of Erasmus and More.

This emergent humanism possesses, if I am right, its own doctrine of the logos, asserts in a radical way that the human world and the world of language are the same. It does not much matter, after all, whether or not it preaches this doctrine in the desert. For an end to the estrangement between humanistic study and the culture surrounding it on all sides cannot arrive until that culture awakens to discover that without some vision of the world in language it is not a culture in any genuine sense, that the loss of the vision is ultimately a disabling loss, and that a society alienated from the world of its discourse is alienated not from humanistic study but from its own essential nature.

INDEX

Abrams, M. H., 62-63, 166
Addison, Joseph, 128
Alkon, Paul, 58n, 155, 160
Aquinas, St., 82
Aristotle, 6, 12, 19-20
Augustine, St., 82, 88

Barthes, Roland, 18, 23, 61
Bate, W. J., 175
Beardsley, Monroe C., xii, 6, 9, 171
Blake, William, 7, 48, 62-63
Bloom, Harold, 166
Brady, Frank, 14n
Brooks, Cleanth, 9, 171
Bulwer Lytton, Edward, 75n
Burke, Edmund, xiv, 79-80, 84-85, 90, 120, 128, 145, 151, 158; Reflections on the Revolution in France, 118
Burke, Kenneth, 93-94

Carlyle, Thomas, 170, 174; Heroes and Hero-Worship, 145; Past and Present, 167
Caudwell, Christopher, 11
Chaucer, Geoffrey, Troilus and Criseyde, 58
Coleridge, S. T., 7, 10
Comenius, 169, 173
Courtenay, John, Poetical Review of the Literary and Moral Character of Dr. Johnson, 71-74, 96, 139-40, 155
Crick, Francis, 62
Culler, Jonathan, 18, 43-44

Derrida, Jacques, ix, 16-23, 35, 61-62, 95, 165

Eliot, T. S., 10, 32
Empson, William, ix
Erasmus, 173-74, 179, 181

Fielding, Henry, Tom Jones (as model of "continuous" narrative structure), 3, 14-16, 23, 25, 45, 47-48, 53-54, 60, 62, 136
Fish, Stanley, 16, 132-33
Fitzgerald, Percy, 59n
Froude, James Anthony, 167
Frye, Northrop, ix, 6, 11

Garrick, David, 111, 115-16, 127
Geneva School (phenomenological criticism), 11, 51
George III (meeting with Johnson), 72, 155
Gibbon, Edward, 3, 116-17, 148, 159, 162; The Decline and Fall of the Roman Empire, 3, 148
Gibson, Walker, 132
Goldmann, Lucien, 11
Goldsmith, Oliver, xiv, 90, 101, 103, 117, 120, 124, 127-28, 138
Graff, Gerald, 166-67

Haley, William, 174n
Hartman, Geoffrey, 16-17, 35n, 62, 165, 169, 170n
Hawkins, Sir John, 141
Hogarth, William, 29-30
Holbach, Paul Thiry, Baron d', 75, 149
Holland, Norman, 132
Homer, Odyssey (as archetypal model for Life of Johnson), 13-15, 23, 62

Library of Congress Cataloging in Publication Data

Dowling, William C
Language and logos in Boswell's Life of Johnson.

Includes index.
1. Boswell, James, 1740-1795. Life of Samuel Johnson.
2. Boswell, James, 1740-1795—Technique.
3. Johnson, Samuel, 1709-1784—Biography.
4. Biography (as a literary form)
5. Narration (Rhetoric)
I. Title.
PR3533.B63D6   828'.609 [B]   80-8545
ISBN 0-691-06455-5

William C. Dowling is Assistant Professor of English
at the University of New Mexico and the author of
The Boswellian Hero (Georgia).